ZACH SCHEIDT'S

BIG BOOK

OF

INCOME

ZACH SCHEIDT'S

BIG BOOK

OF

INCOME

WITH PATRICK MCKELVEY

ISBN: 978-1-6212918-7-9

22 21 20 19 18   3 4 5 6 7 8

Published by Agora Financial, 808 St. Paul Street, Baltimore, Maryland
www.agorafinancial.com

Cover and Layout Design: Andre Cawley
Co-Author: Patrick McKelvey
Associate Editor: Alison Glenn

CONTENTS

FOREWORD

"Wealth is the ability to fully experience life."
—Henry David Thoreau

For generations, retirement was the pinnacle of life. If you worked hard and saved harder, any American could live their golden years doing the things they loved most. Many had pensions, generous Social Security distributions and extra savings to live off. It wasn't hard for Americans to live happily, especially in their old age. Vacations to Florida, buying things without worry, and still having plenty to give to their children were standard expectations. Middle-class America had it made.

But not too long ago, things went awry. The pleasant idea of retirement became a figment of the past. Thoughts switched from "How much can we responsibly afford?" to "How are we going to make it through next month?"

Retirement simply isn't what it used to be. Americans between the ages of 55 and 64 have an average of $104,000 in savings. That translates to a paltry $310 monthly payment if invested in a lifetime annuity. Financial advisers say you need to have at least $1 million in savings in order to retire. Fewer than 5% of American households have money like that.

Social Security won't make up the difference, either. Social Security is meant to be supplemental income or act as an insurance policy for those who fall on hard times. It is not meant to be the main source of retire-ment income.

However, 36% of Americans rely solely on Social Security for their retirement. With the monthly check averaging just over $1,300, it's clear why Americans are struggling. What can $1,300 purchase besides basic necessities? It certainly can't cover home payments or unexpected medical bills. It certainly can't let you live life to the fullest.

Those payments aren't expected to rise, either. Since 2010, the cost-of-living adjustment has averaged 1.1% a year. For most, that's only a few dollars a month. Worst yet, by 2033, the Social Security fund is expected to be insolvent. That's just over 16 years from the date this book is published.

It's time to stop ignoring the facts—**America has a full-blown retire-ment crisis**.

Even though the government created this mess, it is clear they are not going to fix it. Denial, corruption and lies have led the American people to fend for themselves.

And that's exactly why I hired Zach Scheidt and why we published this book. As executive publisher of Agora Financial LLC, I oversee some of the biggest and brightest thinkers in the financial world. Over the years, we have done quite well, and I am proud of what our business has become. In 2009, I co-wrote the *New York Times* best-selling book *The New Empire of Debt* with Bill Bonner. Later, I worked extensively on *I.O.U.S.A*, a documen-tary featured in the Sundance Film Festival. Today, we focus on many "fat tail" trends ranging from currency swings to gold speculation and income generation, as you will find in the following pages.

Zach is our resident income guru and has reached out to hundreds of thousands of Americans through his research and monthly newsletter, *Lifetime Income Report*, helping them to generate the income they want to live a more fulfilling life.

Zach came up with the idea to write a book that not only covers the ideas discussed in his newsletter but also presents opportunities you can use to earn more almost effortlessly. In the following pages, you'll find ways to easily generate income without changing your daily routine.

In fact, Zach recently showed readers how to make $9,400 within the last three months. That's enough spending money for a vacation or a down payment on a brand-new luxury car.

One of the most misunderstood concepts is that you need to have savings to retire. This couldn't be further from the truth. A savings account will disappear over time, but the same money put into income-generating assets will build your wealth tremendously. To retire, you need multiple sources of reliable income, and this book provides 47 unique ways to obtain those streams.

This is a book about living the retirement you always envisioned—and how to earn the income you need to do the things you want.

And this book is just the beginning. New chapters are always emerging and never ending. They are what Zach delivers to eager subscribers each and every month.

The retirement crisis will not solve itself, so it is up to you to make the most of what is given. Take this book and take the monthly newsletter to generate the income you need to live the life you want.

A wealthier life lies ahead, and it all starts here.

Addison Wiggin
Executive publisher, Agora Financial

I. CASH FROM COMPANIES

This section is about publically traded companies that distribute cash to shareholders. In order to partake, you must buy shares in the stock market. You can join some opportunities for as little as $20. The more you invest, the greater the payout.

CHAPTER 1:

HOW TO BECOME A "DIGITAL LANDLORD"

"Why does real estate produce so many millionaires?"

If you have ever wondered the easiest way to get rich without developing a new technology or hitting the Powerball jackpot, look no further than the real estate industry.

Across the globe, real estate is the third most popular way billionaires have accumulated their wealth. According to *Forbes*, 129 of the world's billionaires made their wealth in real estate. The only two industries that produced more were retail (146) and finance (148).

This should seem straightforward—having income-producing properties is a great way to earn more and boost your net worth, both through cash flows and value appreciation. Many individuals have become millionaires through real estate investing, and going down that path can still lead to fortunes today.

The only problem is being a landlord takes time and is a huge responsibility. Sometimes, the costs associated with managing and maintaining properties can eat up all of your profits. Wouldn't it be nice to be a landlord without dealing with calls from tenants, fixing broken walls or having to find someone to rent to in the first place?

In this chapter, I'll show you how to get the lucrative benefits of becoming a landlord without having to personally watch over the properties or pay for any maintenance. In fact, I call it being a "digital landlord" because all transactions and business takes place over the internet. Let me explain.

In 1960, Dwight D. Eisenhower signed the Cigar Excise Tax Extension Act. Don't let the name fool you . . . it wasn't just a law forcing people to pay a little extra for a stogie. Buried in its provisions was a new way for individuals to invest in commercial real estate. Before 1960, real estate investments were too risky and expensive for everyday people. Congress changed that by creating a way for investors to pool their money and collectively buy income-producing properties. That helped diversify risk while allowing investors to earn a share of the profits. The instruments President Eisenhower signed into existence are still around today. They're called real estate investment trusts, more commonly known as REITs.

Most REITs trade on the major stock exchanges, just like any other stock. Each share represents an ownership stake in a real estate venture—anything from a single office building to a group of single-family homes or even hospital buildings. REITs earn money by renting out the properties they own or outright selling them. To encourage groups to create REITs, Congress gave them a fairly nice incentive—qualified REITs don't pay a cent in corporate income tax. No matter if the REIT collects income by renting to tenants or through mortgage payments, it doesn't pay a dime on that income. In exchange, the REIT must pay 90% of its (otherwise taxable) income to shareholders.

That gives REITs some of the highest income yields on Wall Street. In fact, the average REIT yields nearly 4%—twice the average yield of the S&P 500. (To say nothing about the ultra-low interest rates on the average savings account or certificate of deposit.) Because shareholders are owners of publicly traded companies, shareholders of a REIT are landlords of the properties the REIT holds. When a business pays rent, the REIT distributes the rent to owners in the form of dividends. By investing in a REIT, you are investing in the property they own without having to do any physical labor or pay for any maintenance.

Finding REITs to invest in can be tricky if you are unsure of what you are looking for. A great source of free information is **REIT.com**. This website provides laws, news, research and reports regarding every REIT in the industry. It also gives the details on different REIT funds that are composed of various companies. This is a great resource to learn more information.

If starting from scratch sounds like a lot of work, you're in luck. In the next section, I will introduce three unique REITs that provide a great opportunity to capitalize on some of the most lucrative properties in America.

CHAPTER 2:

YOUR RARE CHANCE TO LEGALLY "TAX BACK" THE U.S. GOVERNMENT

When it comes to taking Americans' hard-earned cash, no one does a better job than the United States government. Income tax, sales tax, property tax . . . the government takes our money when we make it and spend it.

Wouldn't it be nice to take a payment from the government for a change?

Well, buried in the depths of the equities market is a little-known way to charge the government rent, which results in a quarterly income check for you. It's a great way to earn a solid yield from a tenant you know is going to make its payments.

Let me break it down for you . . .

The U.S. government is the world's largest employer—with a total of 4.2 million employees. Take out the military, and you still have 2.7 million federal workers—more employees than Wal-Mart or McDonald's has worldwide. All of those employees need a place to work, so you'd probably expect the government to own a bunch of office buildings for them. After all, the federal government owns nearly 640 million acres of land . . . about 28% of the total land area in the United States.

The truth is the federal government turns to the private sector for a lot of its office needs, renting space from somebody else just like any other business. At last count, it was leasing over 55,000 properties. Remember, this is the government we're talking about—it doesn't necessarily rent efficiently. With plenty of taxpayer cash available, government employees don't often worry about how much is paid in rent.

Government rental contracts typically stay in place, locking in long-term leases. Plus, these agencies typically pay rent on time. In order to collect this rent, we have to turn to the private-sector companies the government uses to find offices for its employees.

MEET UNCLE SAM'S LANDLORD

Government Properties Income Trust (NYSE: GOV), as the name would suggest, is a real estate investment trust that owns and invests in properties that are leased to government tenants. Now, I don't mean some local police department or bingo hall from the '70s . . . GOV's tenants include agencies such as U.S. Immigration and Customs, the FBI, the CDC, the FDA and the Department of Homeland Security.

Just check out the complete list below:

Tenant list

TENANT	RENTABLE SQ. FT	% OF TOTAL RENTABLE SQ. FT.	% OF ANNUALIZED RENTAL INCOME
U.S. Government:			
1. U.S Customs & Immigration Service	718,169	6.7%	11.6%
2. Internal Revenue Service	1,041,806	9.7%	8.7%
3. U.S. Government	406,388	3.8%	5.0%
4. Federal Bureau of Investigation	304,257	2.8%	3.5%
5. Department of Justice	221,701	2.1%	3.1%
6. Department of Veterans Affairs	295,172	2.8%	2.9%
7. Centers for Disease Control	297,890	2.7%	2.5%
8. Defence Intelligence Agency	266,000	2.5%	2.2%
9. Department of Homeland Security	125,153	1.2%	2.0%
10. Social Security Administration	189,645	1.8%	1.9%
11. National Business Center	212,996	2.0%	1.9%
12. National Park Service	166,745	1.6%	1.9%
13. Department of Energy	220,702	2.1%	1.9%
14. U.S. Courts	115,366	1.1%	1.8%
15. Natural Resource Center	150,551	1.4%	1.5%
16. Department of Health and Human Services	128,645	1.2%	1.4%
17. Drug Enforcement Agency	147,955	1.4%	1.3%
18. National Archives and Record Administration	352,064	3.3%	1.3%
19. Bureau of Land Management	154,280	1.5%	1.1%

	RENTABLE SQ. FT	% OF TOTAL RENTABLE SQ. FT.	% OF ANNUALIZED RENTAL INCOME
20. Department of State	89,058	0.8%	1.1%
21. U.S. Postal Service	321,800	3.0%	1.0%
22. Defense Nuclear Facilities Board	58,931	0.6%	1.0%
23. Occupational Health and Safety Administration	57,770	0.5%	0.9%
24. Military Entrance Processing Station	56,931	0.5%	0.8%
25. Financial Management Service	87,993	0.8%	0.8%
26. Centers for Medicare and Medicaid Services	78,361	0.7%	0.8%
27. Department of Housing and Urban Development	88,559	0.8%	0.7%
28. Environmental Protection Agency	43,232	0.4%	0.6%
29. Department of the Army	228,108	2.1%	0.6%
30. Food and Drug Administration	33,398	0.3%	0.4%
31. Department of Defense	31,030	0.3%	0.3%
32. Bureau of Prisons	51,138	0.5%	0.3%
33. Equal Employment Opportunity Commission	19,409	0.2%	0.2%
34. Small Business Administration	8,575	0.1%	0.1%
35. Executive Office for Immigration Review	5,500	0.1%	0.1%
36. Non Government	10,080	0.1%	0.1%
37. Department of Labor	6,459	0.1%	0.0%
Subtotal U.S. Government	6,781,817	63.5%	67.0%

TENANT	RENTABLE SQ. FT	% OF TOTAL RENTABLE SQ. FT.	% OF ANNUALIZED RENTAL INCOME
State Government:			
1. State of California — six agency occupants	416,852	3.9%	4.2%
2. Commonwealth of Massachusetts — three agency occupants	307,119	2.9%	4.0%
3. Commonwealth of Virginia — seven agency occupants	255,241	2.4%	2.3%
4. State of Georgia — Department of Transportation	293,035	2.7%	2.3%
5. State of New Jersey — one agency occupant	173,189	1.6%	1.9%
6. State of Oregon — two agency occupants	199,018	1.9%	1.9%
7. State of Washington — Social and Health Services	111,908	1.0%	1.1%
8. State of Arizona — Northern Arizona University	66,743	0.6%	0.6%
9. State of Maryland — two agency occupants	84,674	0.8%	0.5%
10. State of South Carolina — four agency occupants	121,561	0.8%	0.5%
11. State of Minnesota — Minnesota State Lottery	61,426	1.1%	0.5%
12. State of New York — Department of Agriculture	64,000	0.6%	0.4%
Subtotal State Government	2,154,766	20.1%	20.3%
The United Nations	187,060	1.7%	4.5%
Municipalities	111,595	1.0%	1.0%
146 Non-Government Tenants	879,763	8.2%	7.2%
Subtotal Leased Rentable Square Feet	10,115,001	94.5%	100.0%
Available for Lease	585,963	5.5%	—

These are the organizations that ensure the well-being of the United States and have some of the largest budgets aside from the U.S. military. Big-budget tenants are a great thing if you are a landlord—you can always expect rent when it's due.

Remember, Government Properties Income Trust is a private company that buys the buildings and simply leases them back to the U.S. government. In fact, the government is leasing buildings from GOV in 31 out of the 50 states . . . all the states you see shaded in dark gray on the next page.

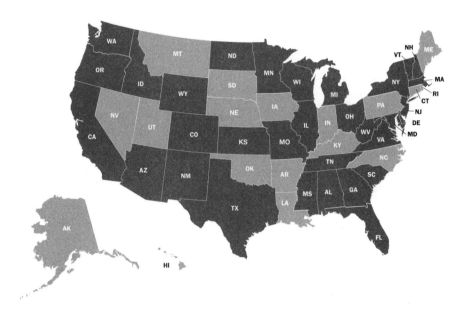

In total, there are 71 properties, filled with thousands of government workers, that are all privately owned by GOV. Every month, GOV rakes in rent payments from all of these buildings and distributes the rent to the company's owners.

Since GOV is publicly traded company, shares trade on the NASDAQ. When you buy shares of GOV, you are buying *actual ownershi*p of the company. It might be a small percentage, but remember, shares of stocks are certificates of ownership. Because GOV operates as a government landlord, when the government makes rent payments, they are paying you, the owner. GOV distributes these payments as quarterly dividends, by law. It's that simple.

Check out the circular flow of funds below.

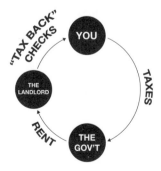

Rent payments are converted into dividends—and GOV has been paying dividends like clockwork since they opened shop in 2009. With an automatic 9.5% yield on your investment, you'll be getting a nice payment from the government within a few months of signing up.

Remember, an REIT must pay out 90% of its income to investors, so GOV gives you a chance to score big dividend payments for cheap—not to mention the potential for tremendous capital gains.

Put it all together, and it's a nearly unbeatable combination. GOV is your chance to regain some of the money you pay in taxes. Pick up some shares and proudly tell your friends that Uncle Sam is paying you rent.

Market Insight: Government Properties Income Trust (NASDAQ: GOV)

Below, you'll find a five-year chart and more descriptions about the company, highlighting their specialization, size, and yield.

Sector: Real Estate	Employees: 570	Dividend Yield: 9.5%
Industry: REIT-Office	Stock Style: Small Value	Price/Earnings: 34

Zach's Income Rating: ★★★★☆

GOV is an exceptional way to generate income by charging the US government rent. As one of the best tenants a landlord could ask for, the US government pays millions to GOV each year which is distributed back to shareholders in the form of a dividend. However, GOV can be quite volatile as a company, and for that reason, earns an income rating of four stars.

CHAPTER 3:

COLLECT A SOLID 5.5% "COPAY" FROM AMERICA'S HEALTH CARE DEBACLE

Universal health care has become a standard government program for many parts of the developed world. This means any citizen within a country that offers universal health care is granted full medical coverage, whether you are homeless or worth millions.

Denmark is a famous example of all-inclusive health care—you've probably heard how medical treatment is free for every citizen. It sounds great in theory, but the Danish people pay for it in taxes. It should be no surprise—this is an expensive program, costing approximately $4,464 per capita per year.

Astonishingly, neither Denmark nor any other European nation has the most expensive health care costs in the world. Leave that statistic to the United States, where the cost of health care is approximately $8,233 per person, nearly double the cost in any OECD nation.

Thanks to greedy companies and successful lobbyists, the medical industry has been able to ramp up revenue at the direct cost of the general public.

As shown in the nearby chart, the United States has by far the most expensive health care costs in the world. With both public and private expenditures, the U.S. spends 2.5 the OECD average—for anything ranging from emergency room visits and prescriptions to yearly checkups. In 2010, the U.S. spent 17.6% of GDP on health care. It's no wonder why so many politicians are calling for reform while others refuse to cooperate and secretly line their pockets with checks from big companies.

U.S. spends two-and-a-half times the OECD average

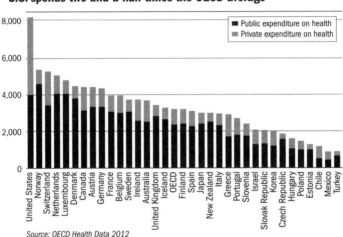

Source: OECD Health Data 2012

With all of that spending, doctors are in high demand. People are constantly going to doctor's offices—and with this you can earn a steady stream of income. Most medical practices rent their properties from larger companies that act as landlords to different medical establishments. Many of these medical landlords are publicly traded companies that investors can buy a stake in. With exorbitant health care costs and the Affordable Care Act forcing everyone into doctors' offices, these companies offer an extremely lucrative way to invest in properties with a constant flow of business.

It's ridiculous that Americans are forced to pay inflated premiums for health insurance and then pay costly fees on top of the premium. Politics aside, here is a way recoup your medical expenses from this faulty system.

HERE IS HOW TO COLLECT YOUR "COPAY"

One of the best ways to profit from America's inefficient health care is by owning **HCP Inc (NYSE:HCP)**, a real estate investment trust that owns assets in five distinct medical industries: senior housing, post-acute/

skilled nursing, life science, medical office and hospital. HCP has been a publically traded company since 1985 and was the first health care REIT selected to the S&P 500. In terms of an income play, HCP is especially profitable, just check out their history of dividend payments:

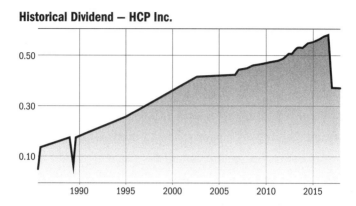

Historical Dividend — HCP Inc.

HCP has an extremely diverse portfolio with over 1,200 medical properties across the globe. With the Affordable Care Act bringing insurance to millions of previously uninsured individuals, the demand for health care services has increased tremendously. HCP is in a position to profit from this increasing demand in a couple of ways. While they own properties that serve various demographics, their largest segment is in senior housing. Take a look at the chart below:

HCP, Inc. property statistics

1,215 TOTAL PROPERTIES

311	Post Acute/Skilled
130	Senior Housing RIDEA
401	Senior Housing NNN
233	Medical Office
124	Life Science
16	Hospital

Source: hcpi.com

It's HCP's stake in senior housing that is poised to profit from the baby boomers' retirements in the next few decades. For those born between 1946 and 1964, senior adulthood is a period of life that exhibits three times the amount of health care spending compared with all other stages of life. As the baby boomers retire, there will be a shift in demographics — the elderly will make up 20% of the population in 2029, compared to 14% in 2012. That means there will be a much greater need for senior housing, and HCP is here to supply that demand.

HCP owns high-quality buildings in attractive locations. In fact, they have $21 billion worth of real estate with tenants that all pay rent. They have increased revenue year over year and maintain a dominant market share as one of the largest health care REITs. Currently, their market cap is around $13 billion, and they pay out a 5.5% dividend—more than twice the income you can expect from the S&P 500.

The way I see it, this is like collecting your very own "copay" from America's inflated health care budget. Simply buy enough shares, and you can easily cover your yearly copays. Let's say you go to the doctor once every 2 months, with a $40 copay each visit. You would need $240 in extra income to cover those payments. An investment of $4,000 would cover those yearly costs, with the added expectation of capital gains.

That's my kind of "copay"! And if management stays true to company ideals, this dividend will only increase further.

It is obvious that the medical system in America is a mess, but HCP is a way you can get a stream of income from the government's inefficiencies. The Affordable Care Act has given millions insurance, which has increased the demand for health care across the country. Additionally, HCP has a large portfolio of senior housing across America that will be provided with a stable flow of tenants as the baby boomers look to retire. If you want to make a profit off of America's health care debacle, I recommend picking up shares of HCP today.

Market insight: HCP Inc (NYSE: HCP)

Below, you'll find a five-year chart and more descriptions about the company, highlighting their specialization, size, and yield.

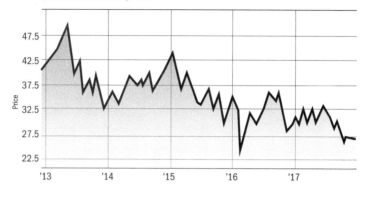

Sector: Real Estate	Employees: 270	Dividend Yield: 5.5%
Industry: REIT-Healthcare	Stock Style: Small Value	Price/Earnings: 24

Zach's Income Rating: ★★★★★

HCP is a best-in-class healthcare REIT that allows investors to profit from the medical debacle taking place in the US. Profits are expected to grow as baby boomers age, and their trend of increasing dividend payments is looking to continue. For these reasons, HCP is a five star opportunity.

CHAPTER 4:

EARN A ROYALTY ON EVERY MAJOR FINANCIAL TRANSACTION IN THE WORLD

Take a look at this nondescript building located in Secaucus, New Jersey:

It's bland and boring and doesn't attract much attention from those who pass by.

To most, it looks like a regular old warehouse. Surprisingly, this boring structure is actually one of the most important buildings in the world. It's not a national security center; it's not a political meeting place and it does not lead to an underground safe house that could save the human race in case of a catastrophe.

So what secret does this mundane building hold? Well, this building is at the epicenter of almost every major financial transaction that takes place in the world. Without it, most modern banks would not exist, and the financial system as we know it would collapse. Simply put, this building holds the servers for the NYSE, the Nasdaq and nearly every major bank on Wall Street.

The building on the previous page is **Equinix Inc.'s (NYSE:EQIX)** NY4 data center and is a modern wonder of the financial world. It's located a few miles from downtown Manhattan and processes every trade, order and transaction on every major stock exchange.

Roughly 9.6 million messages are sent through its fiber-optic cables every second, and trillions of dollars pass through its doors every day. But the NY4 is not just home to the NYSE and Nasdaq...Other major tenants include the Chicago Board Options Exchange, ICAP, IEX and Bloomberg.

To give you an idea of how valuable the NY4 is, in order to get inside access to the servers, you have to pass through five separate security checkpoints, including palm-print scanning, pin-number entry and constant video surveillance. The building has an ultrahigh-tech cooling system that maintains a stable temperature in order to keep the building running 99.9999% of the year. In case of a power failure, the NY4 has thousands of batteries to provide eight minutes of electricity while 18 backup generators the size of freight trains get warmed up.

NY4 is one of Equinix's most valuable properties, but it's not the only property under their operation. In fact, Equinix is considered a REIT and has 145 data centers around the world. They have more than 8,000 customers, including tech giants such as Amazon, Verizon, Microsoft, Netflix, Facebook and LinkedIn. **Figuratively speaking, the internet or modern world would not exist without Equinix and their data centers.**

Best of all, you can become a part owner of Equinix and claim a share of their lucrative dividend. Remember, as a REIT, Equinix must pay out 90% of their earnings by law. That means every time its tenants pay rent, you get cash in the form of a dividend. But it's not just the dividend that is attracting investors.

Had you bought Equinix in February 2003, you would be looking at 12,033% gains on your investment. Those are returns money managers dream of. Year after year, Equinix continues to add properties to their list of assets and make the company more valuable for shareholders.

It is no wonder Equinix is such a hot company. Their business model has made them extremely valuable, which is reflected in their stock price. They currently have a $35 billion market cap and pay a 1.8% dividend. As a REIT, whenever the NYSE or Nasdaq pays rent to Equinix, Equinix returns the payment to investors in the form of a dividend. As long as Equinix maintains their positive relationships with banks, stock exchanges and hedge funds, you can be sure to expect this income stream for years to come.

Remember, Equinix houses the world's major stock exchanges and servers for the largest tech companies in the market. They take their business very seriously and have become one of the best REITs in the world. Investors have made money hand over fist with Equinix, and I expect their success to continue with the expected cash flows coming from their big-name clients. I recommend buying shares of Equinix and claiming rent from their tenants today.

Market Insight: Equinix Inc (NASDAQ: EQIX)

Below, you'll find a five-year chart and more descriptions about the company, highlighting their specialization, size, and yield.

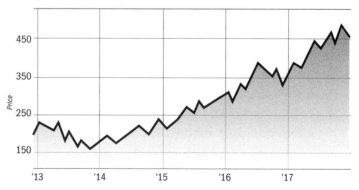

Sector: Real Estate	Employees: 5,042	Dividend Yield: 1.8%
Industry: REIT-Diversified	Stock Style: Large Growth	Price/Earnings: 148

Zach's Income Rating: ★★★★☆

Equinix owns buildings that are an integral part of modern society. Whether you look at the NY4 data center or the facilities that hold Facebook servers, each is a priceless operation which gives Equinix its value. Shares are a little pricey when compared to earnings, but Equinix has solid growth potential and their dividend should increase over time. Therefore, Equinix earns a four star rating.

CHAPTER 5:

COLLECT 12 CHECKS
PER YEAR BY "BACKING"
THE U.S. MILITARY BUDGET

Nuclear submarines . . . unmanned drones . . . missile-destroying lasers . . .

It sounds like the making of a Hollywood movie, but actually they are ways U.S. defense spending could bolster your retirement.

The U.S. spends $600 billion a year on our military, and most of it comes out of taxpayers' pockets. While some of the money goes to pay and feed our troops, the majority of the cash ends up in the hands of U.S. corporations—the kinds that develop new-age heat-seeking weapons and state-of-the-art defense systems.

While many condemn the U.S. military budget, today I'd like to show you how to profit from the hefty spending.

Most of the government contractors that receive money to develop new technologies are publically traded companies that you can buy on the stock market that pay substantial dividends supported by the U.S. government. These companies receive a large share of the U.S. military budget, which means they are constantly generating revenue even if the economy starts to slide.

In this chapter, I would like to show you three of the largest and most advanced companies the U.S. government uses to develop weapons and defense mechanisms that you can use to generate income.

Each is a unique opportunity with different specializations, so take advantage of all three to capture all segments the government invests in . . .

NO. 1: A HEAT-SEEKING OPPORTUNITY THAT PAYS A DIVIDEND

Based out of Waltham, Massachusetts, **Raytheon Co. (NYSE:RTN)** is one of the largest Department of Defense contractors and is a critical supplier of missiles and guided weapons. Raytheon was founded in 1922 as a small refrigerator company, but has since grown into company worth over $54 billion with 61,000 employees worldwide.

Raytheon's roots as a military supplier go all the back before World War II, when British authorities secretly presented U.S. officials with a new form of technology called the "magnetron," which generated microwaves for radar detection. The U.S. government searched for a company that would be capable of producing magnetrons for ground stations, boats and aircraft. In 1940, Raytheon was granted the government contract for producing these radar devices. Over the course of the war, radar became standard technology because of its ability to provide situational awareness, and Raytheon was the top producer of these devices. Following the war, Raytheon invented the guided missile and was given extensive contracts for more unique weapons by the U.S. government.

Since WWII, Raytheon has been a pioneer in weapons development and has provided extensive technologies for the U.S. government. Recent examples include the Patriot defense missile system, the Javelin missile and even the Tomahawk cruise missile. Following the end of the Cold War, many defense companies—such as E-Systems, Texas Instruments and Hughes Aircraft Co.—went out of business, and Raytheon bought up their assets. Raytheon also acquired the underwater torpedo business of Honeywell and is now the sole supplier to the U.S. Navy of the MK 54 torpedo and MK 48 submarine-launched weapon.

Besides their weapons business, Raytheon has a plethora of surveillance and radar programs—holding true to their original roots. Their Space Tracking and Surveillance System has the ability to shoot missiles down at almost any stage of their flight path and can destroy satellites in orbit, while their cybersecurity division is one of their fastest-growing units. Raytheon is a total package when it comes to national security—both on the offensive and defensive sides of the game.

Raytheon's Tomahawk Cruise Missile. Source: Wikicommons

Raytheon has built its business as a "high-reliability organization" and strives for perfection at every level of the institution. For over 90 years, Raytheon has been designing and selling ultra-high-performance products to very demanding customers. Every time Raytheon sells a $1.59 million missile, you can claim your piece of the profit.

Now is the time to get in on this stalwart defense company.

NO. 2: BECOME PARTIAL OWNER OF A B-21 STRIKE BOMBER

The second company I would like to introduce is **Northrop Grumman (NYSE:NOC)** based out of Falls Church, Virginia. Northrop Grumman was founded in 1994 by the merger of two iconic aerospace giants, Northrup and Grumman. The company's roots stretch to before World War II, when the original Northrup helped the U.S. Air Force develop its night-fighter program. At the same time, Grumman designed the Navy's Cat series of aircraft that helped defeat the Japanese in the Pacific theater.

F6F Hellcat. Source: Wikicommons

Today, Northrup Grumman employs 65,000 workers around the globe and is one of the leading designers of military aircraft for a number of countries. They are the current designers of the B-2 stealth bomber and were recently granted a $42 billion contract to produce the fifth-generation B-21 Strike Bomber that is capable of deploying thermonuclear weapons. Northrop estimates they will produce 175–200 bombers, at a price tag of $550 million each. Northrup also designs unmanned aerial vehicles, submarine drone launchers and biometric security systems.

Besides airplanes and bombers, Northrup produces some of the most cutting-edge defense technology available. They've created a new-age sonar called the Light Weight Wide Aperture Array fiber-optic interferometer, which is used on submarines and in harbor defense. Essentially, it's an underwater listening device that will efficiently detect enemy submarines and other unknown threats.

Northrop is a government favorite when it comes to choosing a contractor for certain military projects. If you check out the Department of Defense's website, you can see which companies are awarded contracts above $7 million. Almost every day, Northrup is on the list—either getting extensions or extra projects to boost their revenue.

Remember, buying shares of companies is the same thing as buying ownership. If you buy shares of Northrup Grumman today, you will get to experience the steady flow of income associated with their long-range bomber deal. With 200 predicted orders at $550 million each, Northrup could make upward of $110 billion in revenue just from one product. It's time to claim your income today.

NO. 3: A JUMBO JET MAKER WITH A LONG RUNWAY OF CASH

Just like Raytheon and Northrup Grumman, **Boeing Co. (NYSE:BA)** can trace its roots to the early 20th century when William Boeing, a Yale dropout, started an airplane factory in 1910. Today Boeing is one of the best aviation companies around—an investment in the early 1960s would have yielded a 16,000% return on your money.

Most people know Boeing for their commercial aircraft, which take passengers all over the world. If you have flown in an airplane in the last 20 years, you have undoubtedly set foot in a Boeing passenger jet. While Boeing essentially splits the entire commercial airline market with Airbus, many people are unaware that Boeing has a significant market share in defense, space and security. Of the $90 billion that Boeing brought in in 2015, $30 billion was from their defense segment.

AH-64 Apache. Source: Wikicommons

Boeing's military aircraft range from the famous B-52 bomber to the Army's Apache attack helicopter. They even produce the F-15 fighter jet, which is the world's most popular military fighter, and the P-8A Poseidon, which is a sea-control and anti-submarine warfare aircraft. The Poseidon can detect submarines from long distances away and even drop flying torpedoes on its target.

Boeing is an $168 billion company that employs 161,000 people around the world. This Chicago-based company is a market leader in aviation and will continue to be on top of the industry for years to come. They currently pay a 3% dividend and have been consistently growing revenue and income—which is remarkable for a company of its size. Invest today to be handsomely rewarded.

So there you have it—three companies that provide our military the support and supplies they need, which you can profit from. **If you invest in all three companies, expect to receive 12 checks a year**.

Remember, these companies get most of their revenue from the U.S. government, and military spending is not going to decrease significantly anytime soon. These are three top-of-the-line defense companies that offer a lucrative way to profit from U.S. military spending.

Market Insight: Raytheon (NYSE: RTN)

Below, you'll find a five-year chart and more descriptions about the company, highlighting their specialization, size, and yield.

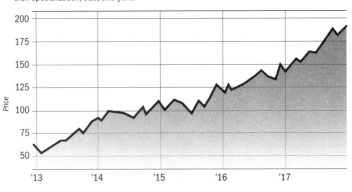

Sector: Industrials	Employees: 61,000	Dividend Yield: 1.7%
Industry: Aerospace & Defense	Stock Style: Large Core	Price/Earnings: 25

Market Insight: Northrop Grumman (NYSE: NOC)

Below, you'll find a five-year chart and more descriptions about the company, highlighting their specialization, size, and yield.

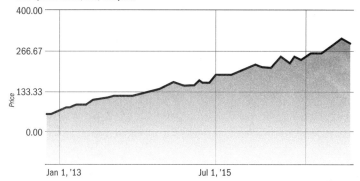

Sector: Industrials	Employees: 65,000	Dividend Yield: 1.3%
Industry: Aerospace & Defense	Stock Style: Large Core	Price/Earnings: 22

Market Insight: Boeing Co (NYSE: BA)

Below, you'll find a five-year chart and more descriptions about the company, highlighting their specialization, size, and yield.

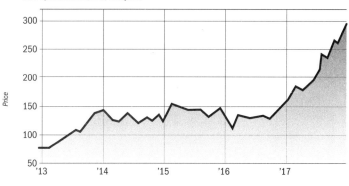

Sector: Industrials	Employees: 161,400	Dividend Yield: 20%
Industry: Aerospace & Defense	Stock Style: Large Core	Price/Earnings: 26

Zach's Income Rating: ★★★★☆

These three companies are defense titans. They receive a large portion of the US military budget, which comes out to a whopping $600 billion a year. Raytheon, Northrup Grumman, and Boeing have all been around for ages and their dividends have attractive yields. The future is bright—and for that reason, each company receives a four star rating.

CHAPTER 6:

10-86 PAYBACK PLAN: HOW TO MAKE BIG OIL "PAY" FOR YOUR GASOLINE (AND MORE!)

What you're about to learn is known by the few who take advantage of it as the "10-86 Gas Pump Payback Plan."

It's an ingenious way to make Big Oil pay your gas bill each and every month that came about during Ronald Reagan's presidency. Sounds amazing, right? Well here is how you can get into these plans as soon as today—and start receiving paybacks from Big Oil.

Oil companies primarily stick to extracting oil and gas from the ground. Some refine it. Some even store it. But that's where their job ends. They leave it to others to figure out how to get it where it needs to go.

One of the safest, fastest and most reliable ways to move oil is through pipelines. However, building pipelines is a real pain. You have to deal with geographic challenges and, of course, the legal challenges—from the individual districts you want to build through all the way up to the navigating the Environmental Protection Agency. Then after all that, you still need to take care of construction.

Frankly, the initial costs outweighed future benefits, so Big Oil didn't want to take the risks involved. That's where Reagan's 10-86s come in. The Reagan administration knew this infrastructure was important but wanted to leave it in the hands of private businesses. They convinced Congress to add a loophole to tax laws, effectively creating master limited partnerships.

Reagan signed the law in October 1986—which is why we call them 10-86 companies.

Here's how it works: In exchange for putting up tons of money upfront to build the pipelines, 10-86 companies get lucrative tax breaks down the road. It's a great deal for them, because once a pipeline is built, there are few ongoing costs. Instead, they receive a lot of income—the money Big Oil companies pay the pipelines to ship their products.

Thanks to the tax incentives, the 10-86s pay zero corporate taxes on that income.

That's right—all that incoming cash cannot be touched by the IRS.

The catch is that 10-86s must pay out a large portion of that income to unit holders (basically the same as shareholders). Not surprisingly, a majority of the unit holders are the Big Oil companies themselves. But they are also available to investors through the regular stock markets, where they trade just like stocks.

Not only can they pay large distributions, but they are forced to do so. At least 90% of their profits must go back to shareholders. Because of this extraordinarily high payout ratio, 10-86s sport extra-high yields.

With the advent of American fracking, pipeline companies are in hot demand. I recommend buying into the following companies to get a piece of the action. They are fast growing and offer some of the highest dividend yields in the market.

Here's a list of my favorite 10-86 Plan companies . . .

ENTERPRISE PRODUCTS PARTNERS (NYSE: EPD)

Perhaps the largest of all pipeline plays, Enterprise Products Partners boasts a $54 billion market cap with a **6.8%** dividend. For a company of that size, the dividend is one of the best, in terms of safety. You can find a map of their pipelines on the next page.

Enterprise Products Partners Asset Map

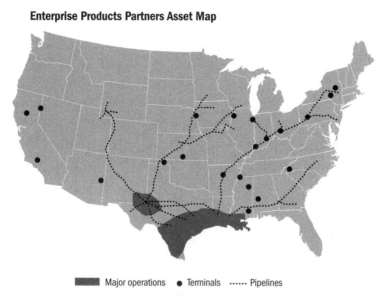

Major operations   ● Terminals   ⋯⋯ Pipelines

ENERGY TRANSFER PARTNERS (NYSE: ETP)

This all-inclusive midstream play has one of the highest dividends in the market, at **14.1%**. This company is a bit smaller than Enterprise Products Partners but has a higher dividend in exchange for that risk. Energy Transfer Equity recently merged with Sunoco Logistics Partners to form one of the most premier midstream companies in the world. They currently pay a **14.1%** dividend with a $19.2 billion market cap. Check out their asset map below.

Energy Transfer Partners Asset Map

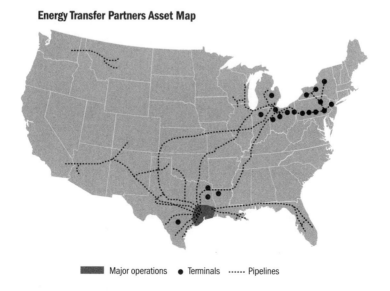

Major operations   ● Terminals   ⋯⋯ Pipelines

MAGELLAN MIDSTREAM PARTNERS (NYSE: MMP)

This midstream play is a cut above the rest because of their strategic placement of pipelines and terminals. Magellan Midstream Partners focuses primarily on refined products, which means they ship goods ready for consumption. What makes them valuable is that they have access to 50% of U.S. refineries, with pipelines running over 9,500 miles. Besides having a dominant share of the refined products market, they pay a **5.3%** dividend.

Magellan Midstream Partners Asset Map

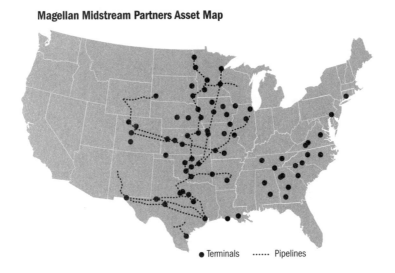

● Terminals   ······ Pipelines

Depending on how much gas you use, simply buy enough shares of these companies to cover your bill each month. Let's say you fill up two or three times a month, which should come out to be $100, depending on the type of car you own. That means in order to cover your yearly bill, you should expect to put in a $20,000 investment. Then let your money grow while collecting dividends along the way. This way, your money works for you, rather than sitting idle in a bank account or certificate of deposit.

While these companies offer some of the best yields on Wall Street, the oil market is volatile and share prices can swing dramatically. Additionally, this strategy requires a substantial initial investment if you want to cover hundreds of dollars in gas each month. However, these pipeline plays are solid companies and the future is bright for American oil.

Market Insight: Enterprise Product Partners (NYSE: EPD)

Below, you'll find a five-year chart and more descriptions about the company, highlighting their specialization, size, and yield.

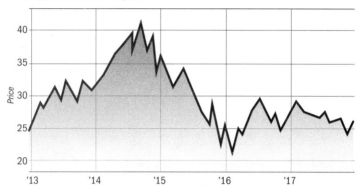

Sector: Energy	Employees: –	Dividend Yield: 6.8%
Industry: Oil & Gas Midstream	Stock Style: Large Value	Price/Earnings: 20.0

Market Insight: Energy Transfer Partners (NYSE: ETP)

Below, you'll find a five-year chart and more descriptions about the company, highlighting their specialization, size, and yield.

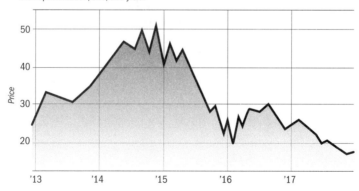

Sector: Energy	Employees: –	Dividend Yield: 14.1%
Industry: Oil & Gas Midstream	Stock Style: Large Value	Price/Earnings: N/A

Market Insight: Magellan Midstream Partners (NYSE: MMP)

Below, you'll find a five-year chart and more descriptions about the company, highlighting their specialization, size, and yield.

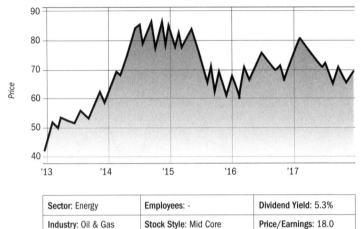

Sector: Energy	Employees: -	Dividend Yield: 5.3%
Industry: Oil & Gas Midstream	Stock Style: Mid Core	Price/Earnings: 18.0

Zach's Income Rating: ★★★★☆

While these companies offer some of the best yields on Wall Street, the oil market is volatile and share prices can swing dramatically. Additionally, this strategy requires a substantial initial investment if you want to cover hundreds of dollars in gas each month. However, these pipeline plays are solid companies and the future is bright for American oil.

CHAPTER 7:

HOW TO PLAY THE MODERN-DAY GOLD RUSH . . . AND GET PAID WHILE DOING IT

Do you own gold or precious metals?

Many financial advisers recommend owning gold as a form of insurance for your wealth. For the most part, I agree with their logic. Gold performs well in certain economic environments because it is a finite resource and has inherent value to humans.

For example, gold is a great inflation hedge and performs well when interest rates are low or enter negative territory. Gold is also a safe haven in times of distress, and people gravitate toward precious metals in general when there is political instability or market turmoil.

All of these factors will cause the price of gold to rise, but only when the factors are in gold's favor. As a long-term investment, gold has no yield and does not provide cash flow, which does not make it good for generating income. Gold does not distribute dividends and will not pay the bills when the mortgage comes due.

Fortunately, there are ways around this dilemma, offering you a chance to profit from the gold market while collecting income along the way. In the next two sections, I'll share unique ways to invest in gold that allow individuals to bring in some serious income.

HOW TO STRIKE IT RICH WITH A DIGITAL GOLD MINE . . . AND COLLECT ROYALTIES ON EVERY OUNCE

There is a little-known way that gold mining companies raise money without contacting banks, venture capitalists or other big-name miners. They are a special type of company that gives miners the money they need in return for a large percentage of the gold they excavate from the ground.

These companies are some of the most profitable businesses you can invest in because they keep costs low while receiving precious metals at an extremely discounted rate. They are called streaming companies (or precious metal royalty plays), and they have given investors decent returns even while the price of precious metals falters.

The secret behind streaming companies is they merely finance the miners and do not take on any operational risk associated with mining. They don't worry about environmental permits or disasters, purchase new bulldozers or tend to faulty blasting situations. They are simply front offices with a few desks that collect receipts for the mine's haul for the day. Streaming companies are a great investment for individual investors interested in precious metals because of their low-risk profile and ability to generate returns even if the price of the underlying asset begins to fall.

Say you are interested in a certain mine because you have reason to believe there are large deposits in the ground. This particular mine is owned by Barrick Gold, but was financed by a streamer. When it comes time to invest, you can put your money in Barrick, or you can invest in the streaming company that provided the funding for Barrick to start the mine.

No matter which company you choose, you will see returns associated with the mine you are interested in. However, the streamer is the better choice for a couple of reasons. The biggest benefit in buying the streamer is that you are protected in case Barrick files for bankruptcy.

Remember, the streaming company provided the funding for Barrick in terms of debt, which means that the streamer is first in line for any collateral in case of bankruptcy. As a shareholder of the streaming company, the collateral from Barrick's bankruptcy would contribute to capital gains. On the other hand, if you owned shares of Barrick, you would most likely lose all of your money.

One of the best streaming companies out there is **Franco-Nevada Corp. (NYSE: FNV)**, based out of Toronto, Canada. Its portfolio consists of approximately 340 properties in various stages of development, from exploration to production. This includes geologists searching for the best places to mine, construction of the mine and actual excavation.

Compared with the biggest name gold miners in the world, Franco-Nevada has significantly outperformed even when the price of gold was on a steady decline. Take a look at the chart below:

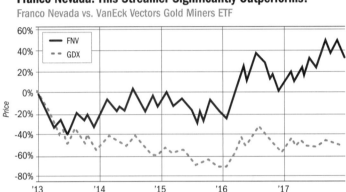

Franco Nevada: This Streamer Significantly Outperforms!
Franco Nevada vs. VanEck Vectors Gold Miners ETF

As you can see, Franco-Nevada was not affected by the fall in the price of gold that started in 2011 like the other major miners were. The VanEck Vectors Gold Miners ETF is a collection of the largest gold mining companies in the world, and their trend represents the typical pattern for big-name companies such as Barrick Gold or Goldcorp. An investment in Franco-Nevada during that time would have not only saved you from losing money, but also brought significant returns. Again, this is due to the streaming business model.

While most miners are currently posting negative returns and margins, Franco-Nevada remains profitable for shareholders. It is an $14 billion company with little debt and only 29 employees—a handful of geologists, financial analysts and a management team. With low operational costs, Franco-Nevada makes a great choice for investing in gold. On top of it all, it pays a 1.2% dividend.

Whether or not gold rises in value, streaming companies are a great investment if you want exposure to precious metals. Their low-cost business model and access to cheap precious metals make them extremely profitable and allow them to distribute cash to shareholders while appreciating in value. I recommend picking up shares today.

Market Insight: Franco-Nevada Corp (NYSE: FNV)

Below, you'll find a five-year chart and more descriptions about the company, highlighting their specialization, size, and yield.

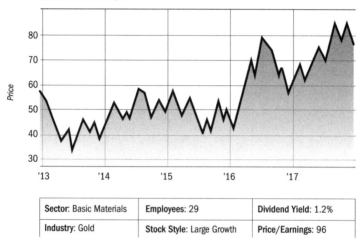

Sector: Basic Materials	Employees: 29	Dividend Yield: 1.2%
Industry: Gold	Stock Style: Large Growth	Price/Earnings: 96

Zach's Income Rating: ★★★★☆

Franco Nevada is one of the best ways to gain exposure to the gold market without taking on any operational risks you would with a miner. Even when gold was slumping from 2011 onward, Franco Nevada brought in positive gains while big name miners lost 50% or more of their value. Their lucrative business model makes gold an attractive investment no matter what economic environment. For these reasons, Franco Nevada earns a 4 star rating.

THE 7.5% GOLD DIVIDEND

Editor's Note: Since we first published this book, this opportunity has fluctuated in yield. This opportunity normally ranges from 5–10%, but due to strong growth, is sitting just under 5%.

I've got an exceptional opportunity for you to collect a huge "gold dividend"—well beyond the typical 1% you'll get from most major miners. As you'll see, this under-the-radar gold company has been paying a dividend like clockwork since 2006. Better yet, the dividend—currently at 4.9%—could head even higher. In the next few minutes, I'll unveil this new opportunity in the gold sphere and why it is not getting the coverage it deserves.

Before I begin, I want you to know one thing—this isn't going to be an endorsement for you to buy gold coins or any other off-the-books gold investment. Instead, you can buy shares of this small company right on the mainstream U.S. markets. Because of its small market cap, this company isn't being covered by any analysts, which means it is less likely to be on the general population's watch list of companies to get in on. However, this company is not one to skip over. Its business model is completely unique, as it does not mine gold, stream gold or have anything to do with exploration and production. On the surface, it doesn't even resemble a gold company. However, it does hold an important key to profiting from the gold coin market.

If you are a gold coin collector, you will know exactly what I am referring to. In 2010, the collectible coin market got turned upside down. One of the largest coin grading services in the world, the Professional Coin Grading Service, made the announcement that they were revamping the coin grading system. They introduced the PCGS Secure Plus service, which doubled the amount of information available to coin collectors and has since become the standard for coin collectors around the world.

Collector Coin Grading Scale

- Original Coin Grading Scale
- New "Plus" Grading Scale Added In 2010

MS/PR-60	No wear. May have many heavy marks/hairlines, strike may not be full.
MS/PR-61	No wear. Multiple heavy marks/hairlines, strike may not be full.
MS/PR-62	No wear. Slightly less marks/hairlines, strike may not be full.
MS/PR-62+	Still slightly above number of marks/hairlines, strike may not be full. Attractive eye appeal for grade.
MS/PR-63	Moderate number/size marks/hairlines, strike may not be full.
MS/PR-63+	Average number of marks/hairlines, strike will be close to average. Good eye appeal for grade.

MS/PR-64	Few marks/hairlines or a couple of severe ones, strike should be average or above.
MS/PR-64+	Very few marks/hairlines or a couple of heavier ones, strike should be average or above. Superior eye appeal.
MS/PR-65	Minor marks/hairlines though none in focal areas, above average strike.
MS/PR-65+	Very minor marks/hairlines though none in focal areas, above average strike and eye appeal.
MS/PR-66	Few minor marks/hairlines not in focal areas, good strike.
MS/PR-66+	Very few minor marks/hairlines not in focal areas, very good strike with superior eye appeal.
MS/PR-67	Virtually as struck with minor imperfections, very well struck.
MS/PR-67+	Virtually as struck with very minor imperfections, very well struck with attractive eye appeal.
MS/PR-68	Virtually as struck with slight imperfections, slightest weakness of strike allowed.
MS/PR-68+	Virtually as struck with very slight imperfections, the strike must be virtually full. Eye appeal must be very good.
MS/PR-69	Virtually as struck with minuscule imperfections, near full strike necessary.
MS/PR-70	As struck, with full strike.

As of May 20, 2016, PCGS has certified close to 33 million coins with a value over $29 billion. According to a survey conducted by the Professional Numismatic Guild and Industry Council for Tangible Assets, PCGS is rated "superior"—the highest rating when compared with competitors. They offer a top-notch grading service that could skyrocket if interest in coin collecting spikes with the increase in precious metal prices.

The thing is PCGS is just a portion of a much larger company called **Collectors Universe (NASDAQ: CLCT)** that provides authentication and grading services for coins, trading cards, autographs, stamps and collectibles. Their other divisions consist of "PSA," or Professional Sports Authenticator, and "PSA/DNA" or PSA/DNA Authentication Services, which both lead the market in grading services. Collectors Universe has a dominant share in the appraisal market and is currently valued at $257 million—with a 4.9% dividend.

If you are a coin collector, you have most likely bought a coin graded by PCGS because of the few competitors that exist in the field. As gold and silver prices grow, the interest in coin collecting will increase and add more revenue for Collectors Universe as more coins are sent in for grading. If you're a coin collector, this is the perfect way to enjoy your favorite hobby and profit at the same time. If you're not a coin collector, this is how you can profit without ever having to buy or sell coins. Now's your chance to step in and collect your 4.9% gold dividend.

Market Insight: Collectors Universe Inc. (NASDAQ: CLCT)

Below, you'll find a five-year chart and more descriptions about the company, highlighting their specialization, size, and yield.

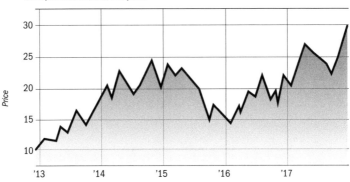

Sector: Industrials	Employees: 302	Dividend Yield: 4.9%
Industry: Business Services	Stock Style: Small Value	Price/Earnings: 24

Zach's Income Rating: ★★★☆☆

As a small cap play, this company is prone to volatile swings and should be considered a riskier investment. Their 4.9% dividend is extremely lucrative and their business has been growing, but I warn you must proceed with caution. Collectors Universe receives a three star rating due to size and risk factors.

CHAPTER 8:

EARN "TOY ROYALTIES" ON YOUR CHILDREN'S FAVORITE CARS AND DOLLS

In 1923, three brothers named Herman, Hillel and Henry Hassenfeld started a company in Providence, Rhode Island. The Hassenfeld brothers were Jewish immigrants from Poland who started off selling textiles and then later moved onto pencils and pencil cases, then crafts and toys.

In fact, the three Hassenfeld Brothers started Hasbro, one of the largest toy makers in the world! This company that started out selling textiles has become the go to choice for Hanukah and Christmas presents alike.

In fact, one of my earliest childhood memories took place in the sleepy farming town of Columbus, Indiana. Growing up, I always looked forward to driving to visit my grandparents for Christmas. We would make the nine-hour drive from Atlanta to Columbus in our "chocolate wagon"—a classic brown station wagon—and usually, we would pass a patch or two of snow along the way.

One special year, we woke up to a white Christmas morning. The landscape was absolutely breathtaking. For the adults at least; for us kids, the snow was just a distraction. The real excitement was in the colorful boxes Santa had left under the tree. That year, my present was a small rectangular box.

When it was my turn, I tore off the paper and found a goofy face with arms and legs attached to his head . . . Nor surprisingly, it was that year that I got Mr. Potato Head!

I spent the rest of the day assembling funny faces with Grandma and Grandpa, and I was just as happy as I could be.

Today, I'm every bit as excited about the holiday season, but my focus is completely different . . .

As a father, I can't wait for my 2-year-old son to open his own Mr. Potato head (or maybe a new Big Bird stuffed animal). My 7-year-old twins will likely be opening Candyland or playing with a new Disney Princess figure or two.

Of course, the big kids will get special presents too, but there's something magical about the younger ones' excitement when the wrapping comes off of the presents. This Christmas morning, I'll be watching my children open their presents and thinking especially about my grandma, who passed away last year.

Grandma got so much joy out of watching her grandchildren and great-grandchildren enjoy the holidays. And this year as my 2-year-old plays with his Mr. Potato Head, I will be remembering her kind smile and my own Mr. Potato Head that I played with at her house so many years ago.

For so many of us, this is what the holidays are really about. Not the materialistic things that we get (or give), but the memories that are attached to these special times. Still, gifts are an important part of the holiday season, and the iconic brands that have been given to children for generations are tied to some very special memories passed down to our loved ones each year.

EARN A ROYALTY WITH THIS LEGENDARY TOY-MAKER

When it comes to making toys, no company comes to mind more than **Hasbro Inc. (NASDAQ:HAS)**. This legendary toy manufacturer is the parent company of some of the most well-known brands that have topped children's wish lists for decades.

Hasbro is one of the world's largest toy-makers, thanks to its ownership of internationally known brands, which include G.I. Joe, The Easy-Bake

Oven, Nerf, Monopoly, Battleship, Candy Land, and the Disney Princess line. Chances are if you have a kid in your life, you've got Hasbro products as well.

The best part is you can use Hasbro to earn a solid stream of income. Here's how . . .

Since Hasbro was founded in 1923 by the Hassenfeld Brothers, it has been the biggest name in the toy business. Hasbro is a publically traded company and you can buy shares from the stock market that pay a 2.5% dividend. If you pick up 66 shares, you are entitled to $152 in yearly dividends.

This dividend is paid four times a year and is transferred right to your bank account, giving you hold-in-your-hand cash (kind of like how their toys are hold-in-your-hand). But before you buy shares of Hasbro, I'd like to explain why they make a good buy.

Hasbro specializes in physical, "under the tree" games and toys, rather than ones that can be downloaded onto a smartphone. Despite all of the brouhaha over children using electronics and leaving traditional toys behind, the actual numbers tell a different story. In 2016, the U.S. toy industry grew 5%. Kids aren't leaving toys behind after all.

As you can see, traditional toy sales are booming! The best part is Hasbro has a dominant share in that market with 10% of domestic toy industry sales.

Annual 2016 U.S. toy industry performance

Super-category	Dollar % change
Games/puzzles	+18%
Dolls	+10%
Outdoor & Sports Toys	+10%
Plush	+6%
Infant/Toddler Preschool Toys	+3%
Youth Electronics	+3%
Vehicles	+1%
Action Figures & Accessories	-1%
All Other Toys	-1%
Building Sets	-3%
Arts & Crafs	-5%

Source: The NPD Group, Inc.

Hasbro remains at the top for a couple of reasons. Hasbro is growing their line of toys in the international sector, and is growing their entertainment and digital businesses through the Discovery Family Network and film tie-ins. In 2016, Hasbro also became the licensed doll maker for Disney Princesses, which helped Hasbro surpass $5 billion in sales for the year.

Hasbro has grown revenues by 12.8% year over year, has increased their net income by 21.9%, and supports their dividend with increasing cash flow. Hasbro is a perfect long-term buy-and-hold company with a healthy 2.5% dividend. I recommend claiming your toy royalties today.

Market Insight: Hasbro, Inc. (NASDAQ:HAS)

Below, you'll find a five-year chart and more descriptions about the company, highlighting their specialization, size, and yield.

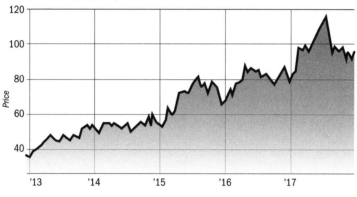

| Sector: Consumer Cyclical | Employees: N/A | Dividend Yield: 2.51% |
| Industry: Leisure | Stock Style: Mid Core | Price/Earnings: 20 |

Zach's Income Rating: ★★★★☆

Hasbro is a great company that has dramatically grown revenue with the addition of their new Disney princess line. With increasing cash flows and stable dividend yield, Hasbro is an attractive investment. And with the increase in the US Toy industry, opportunity continues to unfold. I recommend picking up shares today!

CHAPTER 9:

REVEALED AFTER 127 YEARS: THOMAS EDISON'S SECRET INCOME STREAM

Thomas Edison is one of the most well-known American inventors of the 19th and early 20th centuries. He is most famous for his invention of the light bulb, but most people don't realize he had a plethora of other famous inventions, including the phonograph, motion picture camera and other unique innovations that paved way for the future use of electricity in modern society. Edison was also was also a savvy businessman and used his inventions to create lucrative companies that are still around today—over 100 years since their inception. With the help of J.P. Morgan, Edison merged many of those companies together to start Edison General Electric Co. in 1889.

In 1896, Edison's company was included in the Dow Jones industrial average as one of the 12 founding companies, and it still exists as the General Electric we know today. Most folks don't even know that Edison started GE . . . that's why I call it "Edison's Secret Income Stream."

Today, I'll show you how **General Electric (NYSE:GE)** can bring you hundreds of dollars a year. Like other companies discussed in this book, General Electric is a publically traded company, which means you can buy shares of legal ownership cheaply, quickly and affordably. In fact, you can start your income stream for as little as $30. Here is why I like their business—and why you should too.

General Electric is most commonly known for their household appliances, including washers, dryers, refrigerators and stoves. What most people don't realize is that household appliances only account for a small portion of their total revenue. GE's business goes far beyond washers and dryers in unimaginable ways. From making jet engines for Boeing's 747 to ultrasound devices for cardiologists and even equipment for oil and gas drilling, General Electric does it all.

The pie chart below shows their diversified business segments:

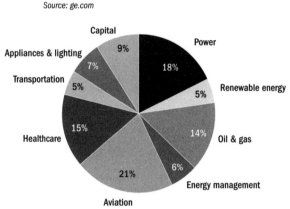

General Electric subdivided by revenue
Source: ge.com

Who would have guessed that power and aviation were their two largest industrial segments? Where GE finds its competitive advantage is in its ability to make quality engines and generators. For power and water, GE produces extremely efficient turbines for natural gas power plants and hydroelectric dams. They also produce the engines that power cruise ships, tankers, airplanes and locomotives.

A few years ago, GE announced a new technology called the "LEAP engine" for commercial airlines, which is expected to revolutionize the aviation industry in the coming years. The LEAP engine is a state-of-the-art product and promises big advances in the airline industry. It is estimated that if a company switches to LEAP engines for their aircraft, it will save $1.2 million a year per plane. That's huge savings for a company of any size.

What makes this engine so good? First and foremost, it is 15% more fuel-efficient than engines currently on the market. Secondly, it is made up of ceramic composites, which are more durable and able to withstand 20% higher temperatures than metal engines. These engines are also designed to stay on the wings of an airplane for eight–10 years before their first overhaul.

GE already has $100 billion in orders for this new engine. That's nearly two-thirds of yearly revenue for all of GE from ONE product. However, there is another reason why I like their business model even more today.

If you look at the chart on Page 54, you will see that GE Capital generated 9% of General Electric's total revenue in 2015. In 2014, that number was significantly higher—GE Capital brought in 28% of General Electric's revenue. That's a 72% drop in year-over-year revenue from their Capital segment, but it's actually a good indicator for investors. Here's why . . .

GE Capital is the financial services unit of General Electric. It provides loans and acts as a bank to various businesses and industries. The thing is, General Electric does not specialize in finance, nor was it started as a financial company, and it's not their expertise. After the financial crisis of 2008, GE Capital suffered tremendously, which in turn has brought down their share price. Simply put, it is a major burden bringing down the company.

However, the reason General Electric is so attractive these days is because they are **selling off GE Capital**. General Electric has decided to sell off their financial assets and restructure to focus on what they are best at—industrial goods and services.

General Electric plans on getting rid of this blemish, and fast. It's not an easy task to sell off a segment worth multibillions. General Electric has already sold off most of GE Capital and announced in August 2015 that they are selling off the final $16 billion to Goldman Sachs, which will mark their exit from the banking business.

All of GE's recent moves are acting in its favor. With more financial assets being sold and restructuring to focus on what they do best, GE's management is making all the right choices. Best of all, you can buy shares of General Electric and collect a royalty that has been paid since the commercialization of the light bulb. In terms of safety, GE has been paying a dividend for over 100 years.

I recommend getting in on Edison's Secret Income Stream and claiming your 3% dividend today.

Market Insight: General Electric (NYSE:GE)

Below, you'll find a five-year chart and more descriptions about the company, highlighting their specialization, size, and yield.

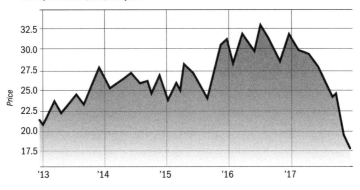

Sector: Industrials	Employees: 333,000	Dividend Yield: 3.2%
Industry: Diversified	Stock Style: Large Core	Price/Earnings: 34

Zach's Income Rating: ★★★★☆

General Electric is one of the best dividend paying companies in the business. They offer a solid yield that has been paid for over 100 years! This company is stable, large, and only looking to grow their business. Therefore, GE earns an income rating of four stars.

Hey, Zach Scheidt stopping in!

I hope you've been enjoying my *Big Book of Income* so far, and have used some of these ideas to boost your daily cash flow.

But I have a favor to ask you...

If you have a second, would you stop by **sites.agorafinancial.com/LIR/BigBookSurvey** and let me know what you think of the book?

I want real feedback telling me what chapters you've used, and how much income you've been able to generate.

Thanks in advance!

Here's to growing your income,

Zach Scheidt

II. THE INTERNET OF INCOME

This section is about different ways to make income through online opportunities. You can start some strategies today with zero startup capital. Some are controversial, and some require a time commitment.

CHAPTER 10:

HAVE YOUR MORTGAGE PAY FOR ITSELF AND EARN $1,061 A MONTH OR MORE

If Americans had the chance to cut one monthly bill out of their expenses, I would guarantee mortgage payments would be at the top of the list. A mortgage, or "death pledge" if translated into French, is one of the largest causes of financial hardship for many hardworking Americans.

Instead of letting your house take the money from your bank account, today I've got a way to have your own home become a money-generating machine. In fact, the income you can generate with this trick could easily cover the average monthly mortgage payment—if not more.

With this trick, you can earn thousands of dollars a month. Whether it's paying off the mortgage, saving for retirement or bumping up the spending budget, this technique can put money in your pocket through a growing trend available through the recent technological revolution.

If you have a spare room or extra property, then this style of income generation might be the perfect solution for paying off bills or adding to your retirement.

Let me show you how it works . . .

For many Americans, the idea of homeownership has gone out the window. With increasing housing costs, renting has become the new norm. If you check out the chart below, you will see how dramatically homeownership has shifted over the last four decades:

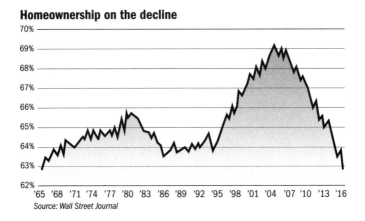

Homeownership on the decline

Source: Wall Street Journal

Following the subprime housing crisis that erupted in 2007, home-ownership rates have gone down and only continue to decline.

This means more people are looking to rent.

Millennials in particular have stopped buying homes as well. There is a growing trend to travel and move from city to city rather than settle in one location. Many millennials also take gap years to explore the world before they get comfortable in the working world. The constant change in addition to massive loads of student debt has caused a steep drop in millennial homeownership. The change in occupied housing units from owner to tenant since the recession can be seen in the chart below:

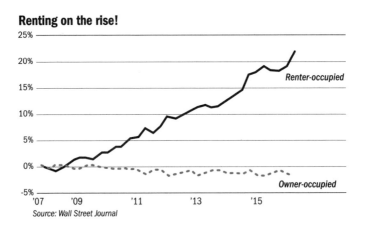

Renting on the rise!

Source: Wall Street Journal

The drop in homeownership rates has made it easy to turn your own properties into cash cows through one website: **Airbnb**.

Airbnb is part of the share economy that lets users list, find and rent lodging in over 34,000 cities across the globe. Airbnb has over 2 million listings you can choose to rent from and averages 500,000 bookings a night. The platform allows individuals to rent a room or even an entire house for a specified amount of time—from a single day to even over a month. Generally, the prices are cheaper than hotels and the services are better, which has attracted the business of millions across the globe. In summer 2015, over 17 million people booked a stay with Airbnb.

Airbnb has made it possible to generate thousands of dollars a month simply by renting out your unused space in your own home. You can easily become a landlord without the long-term commitment of signing tenants. In most places in the U.S., you are legally allowed to rent your home for 14 days or less and not pay a cent in taxes.

Let's take a look at how profitable Airbnb can be for a host. The following is a hypothetical example for two common situations. The first is renting out a room in your own house, the second out an entire second property:

Hypothetical rental income

	Single Room	Whole House
Price per night	$80	$200
Monthly Income Renting on Weekends (8 days a month)	$640	$1,600
Yearly Income Renting on Weekends (8 days a month)	$7,680	$19,200
Monthly Income Renting Full Time (28 days a month)	$2,240	$5,600
Yearly Income Renting Full Time (28 days a month)	$26,880	$67,200

As you can see from this chart, Airbnb can be an extremely lucrative business for those who take advantage. Renting out a single room for $80 a night can net you $640–2,240 a month. Average rates vary from region to region—some places like New York City are going to have higher rates than other locations. In any case, Airbnb offers an easy way to make extra cash from the space you aren't using.

For those uneasy with the idea of letting someone stay in their house, let me walk you through Airbnb's business model. First and foremost, you get to choose who you let rent out your property. Just like customers can leave ratings on places they stay, hosts leave ratings on guests that will impact their ability to rent in the future. When a guest books a room, the host has to accept the reservation before any transactions take place. The host can also cancel the reservation at any time (although it is polite to cancel as soon as possible). This way, the host is in complete control of who they are letting use their space.

Airbnb is a wildly successful business that offers a great way to earn thousands of extra dollars a month that could easily cover the cost of your mortgage. While they try to make things easier by sending a 1099 every tax season (to declare income), laws regarding the share economy vary from state to state. Some areas consider Airbnb residences as hotels under different circumstances, which will affect your ultimate tax rate.

Get acquainted with your local law and figure out if Airbnb is right for you. This lucrative business is a great way to earn a supplementary income that can cover the cost of your mortgage or put thousands of extra dollars in your pocket.

Check out **www.airbnb.com** for more information.

Zach's Income Rating: ★★★☆☆

This is a fantastic opportunity to earn thousands of extra dollars simply renting out a room a few times a month. Airbnb provides the software and support to create a great business that can generate tremendous amounts of income. However, because this opportunity requires effort on the part of the host, and some individuals may still feel uneasy with renters using their property, Airbnb receives three stars.

CHAPTER 11:

HOW MY GRANDMA MADE AN EASY $1,600 A MONTH, AND HOW IT CAN BE EVEN EASIER FOR YOU

Even in her old age, my grandma was just about the most money-savvy person I knew. She often spent her free time doing things she enjoyed — watching the neighbors children (I secretly think she missed us) or knitting items for when the grandchildren came to visit. The best part is my grandma made money doing all of these things. In these next few sections, I'll show how she made thousands of dollars a month doing things she enjoyed, and how it can be even easier for you.

THE EASIEST $1,600 MY GRANDMA EVER MADE

One of the best retirement jobs to pick up extra cash is something you probably haven't considered since high school. Its low-stress, highly lucrative and even a bit of fun. It's also a job that netted my grandma $400 a week working only 24 hours.

What did my grandma do, exactly? Well, she was a baby-sitter. And while that might be off-putting to some, my grandma was raking in an extra $1,600 a month just by watching the neighbors kids while their parents were at work. For the parents, it was cheaper than day care, and they liked the personalized attention their kids were receiving.

During the summer, my grandma typically watched kids four days a week from 9 a.m. to 3 p.m., or 24 hours per week, and made $1,600 a month. It was a low-stress job because she enjoyed spending time with the kids when otherwise she would just be doing things around the house. My grandma was always thrifty, but the extra cash allowed her to save more and splurge on her own grandchildren. Presents were always a little bit nicer come Christmastime, and I think it had a lot to do with her summer baby-sitting gig.

Today, finding baby-sitting jobs is easier than ever. Technology has made it easy to connect potential sitters with families that need child care through an app.

UrbanSitter is an online application that connects families to experienced baby-sitters all across the country. The way it works is simple. Baby-sitters looking for work enter their credentials, and families looking for a baby-sitter can go on the app and search for a sitter that suits their needs. Parents can look at the sitter's profile, which contains reviews from other parents, baby-sitting rates, amount of experience, special qualifications, availability, certifications and the locations in which they are willing to work. Parents can even watch a video profile submitted by the potential sitter to get to know them better before they decide to have an interview.

Parents have the option to post a job opening and screen through sitters that express interest in the position, or browse through available sitters and reach out to them as needed. Parents can sign up and browse for free, but once they are ready to interview a sitter, they must subscribe to a membership, which is $14.95 a month or $99.95 a year. For sitters, there is no membership fee.

Sitters can be paid through cash or check, or on the app itself, which makes it easy for all parties involved. If you are looking to make extra cash, this is a great way to find baby-sitting gigs at your own leisure. You create the hours you want to work and decide how much you charge. There are currently 50,000 baby-sitters working through the app, and the reviews are tremendous. Check out what parents are saying about Urban-Sitter, taken from the company's website:

Booking a baby-sitter used to be a serial process. With UrbanSitter, I can simply go online and I immediately know what my options are for any given evening or weekend.—**Megan M., San Francisco**

UrbanSitter has become one of those services that we absolutely couldn't survive without as parents.—**TJ L., Boston**

I've been consistently impressed at how enthusiastic, smart and qualified the sitters are, especially with special needs kids. But my favorite thing? I can pay with my credit card. No more ATM stops!
—**Jessica S., Boston**

Whether we've got an event far in advance or need a sitter for our weekly date night, UrbanSitter has become our go-to solution.
—**Lance S., New York City**

It's not just parents that are raving about the app. Baby-sitters love how it easily connects them with parents, allowing them to conduct more business than if they didn't have the app. Check out what sitters had to say:

"I'm a huge fan. Sitters are rewarded for professionalism and out-standing child care through parent reviews, which in turn makes it easier to get more baby-sitting gigs as you build a positive reputation on the site."—**Fayette F., San Francisco**

"So glad I found UrbanSitter! Networking is how I've always met great families before, and UrbanSitter makes it that much easier to connect."—**Sarah G., Boston**

I have tried several services to find baby-sitting jobs. I found child care websites to be impersonal and nanny agencies claimed up to 15% of my wages. With UrbanSitter, I can see what personal connections I have with prospective families and keep every dollar I make.—
Kate J., San Francisco

Signing up on UrbanSitter is easy. You begin by setting up a profile and giving details regarding your experience, hourly rates, availability and the areas in which you wish to work. You give a description of yourself as a personal introduction that should describe your education, experience with kids and anything else a parent might want to know. You sign a code of conduct, simply agreeing that you will be transparent, respond to requests and uphold commitments. You then list the times you are available, enter direct deposit information so you can get paid through the app and then you are on your way.

For retired Americans or those looking to work more in their spare time, UrbanSitter is a great, low-stress way to make extra cash in your local neighborhood. The app allows you to directly search for jobs and reach out to families that are interested in child care. If you have extra time, this is a great way to generate a few hundred to over a thousand dollars a month depending on how much time you put in. Give UrbanSitter a try today.

THE MILLION-DOLLAR HAND-KNIT BUSINESS

Another thing my grandma loved to do was make gifts for all of the grandchildren. My grandma was never a TV person, so whenever she had free time she would sit on the couch and knit whatever her heart desired. My friends took a liking to my grandma's creations . . . I once left a blanket at a camp-out, and it's been gone for 35 years. My grandma would also sell her creations when the local church would host a big yard sale, and she would clean up her competitors!

Nowadays, boutique artists and craftsman have an easy way to sell their products without going to the local market or setting up a brick-and-mortar storefront. Through etsy.com, many artists have made a living by selling their products directly over the internet.

If you haven't heard of the website **Etsy**, it's time to listen up. Last year, over 24 million buyers from around the world spend $2.3 billion on Etsy's products, which are supplied by people like you and me.

As a seller, the benefits are awesome. Etsy provides technology to manage your shop on the go and see what kind of people visit your online store. You can even design your own custom site. Etsy provides support over the phone or by email for shop owners, and also has a plethora of articles detailing how to make your business as successful as possible. If you check out the Etsy handbook, you will find hundreds of articles ranging from legal selling advice to growth strategies and even ways to improve your productivity. I've copied the link below.

https://www.etsy.com/seller-handbook?ref=us_sell

In order to sell your items, they must be classified as one of the three categories. Handmade goods, vintage items (over 20 years old) or craft supplies. Once you figure out what you are going to sell, setting up shop is easy. Simply fill out the forms detailing your language and currency, and give your shop a name. Then add the items you wish to sell and set up how you are going to be paid.

When you list an item, you pay a 20-cent listing fee. Then when the item is sold, you pay a 3.5% transaction fee and a payment processing fee of 3% plus 25 cents. The money you earn then appears in your shop payment account. Every Monday, the funds are deposited into your bank account.

The benefits of Etsy are endless. You don't have to pay rent for a store-front, and you can focus most of your time and effort on actually making your items. You can then spend that money on your projects rather than worry about insignificant operating costs.

Through Etsy, some shop owners have brought in more than a million dollars in revenue. Many sellers have become so successful that Etsy has become their main source of income. If you have a hobby like leather-working, knitting, making bird houses or painting, Etsy could be a great way to make extra money while doing the things you love.

If you are interested, check out etsy.com for more information.

Zach's Income Rating: ★★★☆☆

While great sources of income, these techniques require work on the part of the individual. While babysitting was a source of low stress income, it required a time commitment. The same applied to her knitting. While she made money, it took time. Therefore, these opportunities receive three stars.

CHAPTER 12:

THE $35-AN-HOUR JOB ALMOST ANYONE CAN GET

The new "app era" has made it incredibly easy to offer your skills or home without having to go through the traditional means of creating a business. This has allowed millions of people to make money through channels that did not exist a decade ago. For many apps, you simply sign up, pass a background check and start working right away.

In this chapter, I'll show you how to offer up your skills at dog walking. And soon you could be making up to $35 an hour—on your own schedule.

One of the largest companies that brings dog walkers and customers together is **Rover.com**, which is very similar to Airbnb. When you decide you want to look after pets for a stream of income, Rover allows you to choose how you will conduct business. You can walk dogs for various lengths of time, have a pup come stay with you, care for a dog while saying at a customer's house, drop in for a visit or even watch dogs during the workday. Users also get to set their own prices, so it's important to research competitors in order to gain the advantage. Over 1 million rounds of dog-sitting have been booked through Rover, so you can have confidence in their business model.

A more in-demand service that allows dog owners to contacts walkers on the go is Wag. Wag is like the Uber of dog walking and is most prevalent on the West Coast and big metropolitan cities. With this app, dog owners can request walks on a weekly schedule, or ASAP, which will get a dog walker to your house much like requesting an Uber. Wag sends a free lock box in the mail so dog walkers are able to securely walk their customers' dogs while the owners aren't home. Dog walkers can make $20–25 per half-hour or $30–35 per hour depending on the location. Additional dogs are an extra $5 each. For an hour of exercise, $30 isn't a bad deal. Plus, you can schedule as much or as little walking time as you please. Four hours of walking a week (which you should be doing anyway for health reasons) will land you $120 or more. That's an extra $480 a month.

Wag walkers will schedule a free meet and greet in case the owner wants to meet the dog walker before they begin their service. It is a great way for the walker to meet the dog and for the owner to feel comfortable knowing their dog is in good hands. In order to work for Wag, you must be certified, pass a background check and be insured in case of an accident.

There is a quiz that interested dog walkers must complete in order to submit their application. It is to ensure that walkers know basic dog behavior signs and can make the best choices possible when presented with aggressive scenarios. Afterward, there is a phone interview to discuss your experience and availability, followed by a hands-on assessment.

It is recommended all dog walkers carry the following: waste bag to pick up after the dog, citronella spray to ward off any unexpected unleashed dogs, a flashlight, extra water and treats. Before you decide to get into the business, you should be in good enough health to walk for a few hours each day and be familiar with basic training commands. Remember, some dogs can be more rambunctious than others, so it is important to have experience dealing with misbehaving dogs.

If you are interested, check out the following websites for more information:

Rover.com

Wagwalking.com

If you are a dog person, these apps are a great way to make extra money in your free time. $20 for a half-hour walk . . . that's nothing to sniff at. If you are looking for income, it's time to get walking.

Zach's Income Rating: ★★★☆☆

While this opportunity is a great way to make easy money, it requires work on the part of the individual. Watching dogs may be lucrative and enjoyable, but the physical requirements make it difficult for some to partake. This is however, one of the easiest jobs to find, and you can set your own time frame.

CHAPTER 13:

EARN "BLACK MARKET CASH" ON EVERYDAY EXPENSES

Credit cards have been a wonder for modern-day consumers. For those that use them properly, they are a way to earn hundreds if not thousands of dollars on yearly purchases without a cent of added interest.

On top of benefits, those that properly use credit cards typically have the lowest interest rates and best financial profiles when applying for loans. Not only are you more likely to get financing — the loan itself will be cheaper.

Unfortunately, those that spend more than they can afford become trapped in a cycle of high-interest debt from which it is seemingly impossible to break free. This makes credit cards a double-edged sword and has led to their nasty reputation.

In this chapter, I'll show how credit cards can be used to maximize returns on purchases and improve your credit rating along the way. As irresponsible as some Americans get with spending, credit cards are awesome tools that you can use to earn back thousands of dollars on your yearly purchases.

Sometimes you can earn direct cash back. But lots of the time, you'll earn reward points, or what I like to call "Black Market Cash." Whether you're buying airfare, hotels or gift cards, this "Black Market Cash" can go a long way. There is no reason you shouldn't be taking advantage of free money.

Many credit cards offer rewards programs that give users incentives to use that specific card. These rewards will usually be in the form of cash, free airline miles or general rewards points. Rewards will typically range from 1–5% of the total value of each transaction. For the organized spender, credit cards should be used to make the bulk of purchases because you can earn rewards on every purchase. It's free money as long as you make your payments on time with an added layer of financial security. Why take cash directly out of your account when you could earn a 5% bonus by swiping a credit card? As long as you keep track of your expenses, you should have no problem paying off your balance in full every month.

Typically, credit cards fall under one of the following categories:

Standard Credit—The most common type of credit card from banks and financial institutions. Usually, these are no frills, but have no annual fee.

Cash Back—Allows users to earn cash rewards on every purchase. Typically, these cards offer a 1% return.

General Rewards—Users accumulate points through purchases and can apply these points to gifts.

Hotel Rewards—Allows users to accumulate hotel points through general use and bonus points when booking with specific co-branded hotels. For example, earn 1 point for every dollar spent outside of the hotel brand and 5 points spent within the hotel brand.

Airline/ Train Rewards—Similar to hotel rewards, but allows users to accumulate points that can be used for future travel.

Retail Rewards—Allows users to accumulate points through general use with bonus points when used at specific retailers.

Gas Rewards—Typically gives 1% cash back for general purchases and 5% back when purchasing gas.

If you are organized and good with keeping track of expenses, having a credit card in each category can give you an arsenal of double bonuses, ultimately putting more cash into your pocket. If you have the money for the item, why pay cash when credit will give you an instant 1–5% on your purchase?

Here is a simple portfolio of credit cards most people would qualify for that allows for awesome bonuses in nearly any situation.

American Express Blue Cash Preferred—Get 6% back on groceries, 3% back on gas, 1% other purchases. Spend $1,000 in first three months and receive $200 in statement credit. Annual fee of $95.

Discover IT—Discover will match your total cash back on first-year purchases. You also get 5% back in bonus rotating categories such as home improvement stores or restaurants and 1% back on everything else.

Chase Freedom Unlimited—Get 1.5% cash back on every purchase.

Southwest Rapid Rewards—Get 40,000 points if you spend $1,000 in first three months, plus 2 points per $1 spent on Southwest Airlines, 1 point for every other purchase and 3,000 points on the card member anniversary.

Starwood Preferred Guest—Redeem points for free nights. Get 30,000 points if you spend $3,000 in first three months.

This array of credit cards will allow you to maximize bonuses in almost any situation. From travel to groceries and gas, you can earn 1–6% back on any purchase—just use the right card for the right situation. If you don't think you are organized enough to manage several credit cards, fear not. There is a way to easily track and maintain your expenses while maximizing your rewards.

NEVER LOSE ANOTHER DOLLAR IN REWARDS

For those wary of using multiple credit cards, a mobile app called Wallaby takes care of all your worries. Wallaby will track every expense and all available rewards for your arsenal of credit cards.

The way it works is simple. Wallaby has a list of your credit cards and uses your location to determine which credit card should be used to maximize your bonuses.

While you are waiting in line to cash out at the store, simply open Wallaby and your list of credit cards will show up with the points you are able to earn as you are about to purchase. Because credit cards have different incentives and some have rotating reward categories, Wallaby will ensure you are using the card that will give the greatest bonuses. So instead of using the standard cash back card to get 1.5% while dining, Wallaby would inform you that a 5% reward is available on another card.

Wallaby was named a top app by *Money* magazine—and rightly so. It has helped thousands of Americans organize their credit cards and maximize bonuses. Wallaby constantly updates its database so it can always make the best decision when it comes to your cards. No matter if there are new rewards, changed interest rates or increased fees, Wallaby always has the most up-to-date information. Wallaby also uses bank-level protection so you can be sure that your information is completely secure.

If you are unsure of which credit cards to obtain, Wallaby will also recommend a tailored list of cards that fit your spending needs through their WalletBoost feature. This way, you will have the perfect mix of credit cards for all your needs.

Editor's note: Turning credit into cash back or travel miles is advantageous only if you can responsibly use credit cards and pay off the balances in their entirety every pay period. Properly managing your credit cards is one of the most important pieces of modern-day finance. If you don't, you could end up owing 20% or greater interest on your purchases, which would negate any positives coming from rewards points. Even earning 6% back on your grocery purchases will not benefit you if you owe 15% in interest.

Zach's Income Rating: ★★★★☆

As stated before, you should only use credit cards if you are responsible with purchases and can pay off your monthly statement. Paying 20% interest will sink your bank account and credit score. When used effectively, credit cards should be used for the bulk of purchases as you can add thousands of dollars to your pocket each year.

CHAPTER 14:

TURN YOUR DAILY COMMUTE INTO DAILY CASH

The average American's commute to work is 25.4 minutes, according to the U.S. Census Bureau. In this chapter, I'll show you how to take a few of those minutes and turn them into cash, paying for your car plus a little extra along the way. And if you don't work, here is a way to make some money going toward any destination.

Ridesharing, similar to the peer-to-peer lending discussed in other chapters of this book, is a great way to make extra income without changing your daily routine. By taking a passenger with you on your way to work and back home, you can make enough money a month to cover your car payment as well as extra spending money.

The most popular ride sharing programs are Uber and Lyft. Both apps allow people to turn their cars into sources of income by giving neighbors rides. These programs have become a big hit with both people wanting to earn income as well as for those looking to go places. Simply press a button on your phone and a ride shows up to your house within a few minutes. Compared with taxicabs, ride sharing programs are more efficient and also more cost-effective for riders.

You can use Uber or Lyft to make your car pay for itself, but you don't have to work extra hours or change up your schedule to do so. In most cities, these apps have a "going my way" feature that allows drivers to only pick up passengers who are traveling in the same direction.

If you are traveling 25 minutes to work, pick up a passenger going in your direction and you can make $12–15. Do the same thing going home and you can easily cover the cost of your car, making $480 –600 a month just by taking a passenger while keeping your routine the same.

Again, this isn't significantly changing your daily schedule. The person is already traveling in the direction you are going, so you can use this advantage to make money simply driving to work. Of course, the person may be a few minutes away from your destination, and rides might not be consistent, but those extra dollars add up and can be huge in the long run. Uber is available in 758 cities around the world and Lyft is available in most major U.S. cities, so most Americans have the opportunity to partake.

Another added benefit is that you can use these programs as significant tax write-offs. You can write off your insurance, cellphone bill, mileage and any expenses to your car, since they are considered business expenses. Even if you make it all the way to work without picking up a rider, you can write off the miles traveled.

You don't have to have any long-term commitments with these programs. You can test out this strategy for a month and see if it's working for you.

It's safe, too. Just remember that Uber teams up with law enforcement and has a rapid response team that is available around the clock to handle any urgent safety concerns. Riders must register with the service, which means there are no anonymous pickups and everyone's information is transparent.

A close friend of mine drives Uber on his way home from work and generates $1,200 a month. However, instead of selecting the "going my way" direction, he puts in about two–three hours each day after work and some weekend nights. He says the best part about Uber is that you are on your own schedule and can turn the app on and off whenever you please.

But you don't have to work those kinds of hours to make effective income. Simply doing a ride to and from your work can pay off your car bill.

Check out uber.com and lyft.com for more information. Sometimes, these apps will provide car insurance, bonuses and gas cards for hitting certain milestones, which might be more incentive for you to start.

Zach's Income Rating: ★★★☆☆

While Uber and Lyft can cover your monthly car bill simply by driving to work, it will extend your trips and may be a hassle if you are forced to wait for passengers. However, with the "Going My Way" feature, you can drive individuals who are already going in your desired direction. For these reasons, ridesharing earns a three star rating.

CHAPTER 15:

USE YOUR MIND AND BODY TO EARN $275 A MONTH

One of the easiest ways to get extra money is to participate in research studies hosted by your local university or nearby medical facility. You see, scientists and pharmaceutical companies are in constant need of volunteers for research, and if you sign up, these gigs can land you anywhere from a few hundred to tens of thousands of dollars. There are two main options when it comes to research—observational studies and clinical trials.

Observational studies are used to add to the world's current medical knowledge—the type you see that are typically advertised by local universities. Depending on what kind of study you sign up for, you might need to belong to a certain demographic or have a certain medical condition or some specific genetic trait. Some studies have stricter guidelines than others. For example, some studies may ask for females aged 18–65, while some may ask for males aged 18–35 who have smoked at least 10 menthol cigarettes a day over the past year.

Lets consider the following example. A researcher might be attempting to determine what happens to brain waves when you drink coffee before you go to bed. The researcher gets a group of 100 people, divides them in into two subgroups and gives one group regular coffee and the other decaffeinated. The subjects then attempt to sleep while connected to monitors, and the researcher collects the data. By doing this study, the researcher hopes to paint a better picture for scientists and doctors of how our body reacts to coffee before we go to bed. Other examples of observational studies could be virtual reality and touch response, or simply filling out a survey regarding your impressions of certain advertisements.

Usually, simple tests like surveys will land volunteers a couple bucks, or a more involved study will land hundreds of dollars. For the biggest payouts, you might end up lying in a bed for 70 days like a few people did for NASA, in which case they made $18,000. It should go without saying that the more money you are paid, the more time it may require or the higher the potential risk to your health.

Check your local university for listings regarding these kinds of studies. Most have a list giving the basic details and compensation information. Here is an example from New York University's website:

New York University research study opportunities

Study	Lab	Time	Pay
Neural representation of valuation	Glimcher Lab	2 sessions, 2 hrs each	$120 + possible food consumer items
How do we learn to produce new words?	Buchwald Lab	~100 min over 2 sessions	$35 upon completion
How do we make decisions?	Glimcher Lab	90 min	$50 + task learning
Personal memories + Decision making	Phelps Lab	2-day study, 1.5 hrs per day between day 1 and day 2	$15 per hr on day 1, and $25 per hr on day 2, plus bonus of to $60 depending on performance
Sleep and learning study_SoM	SoM	2 hrs sleep + 2 hrs awake	$15 per hour

BECOME THE HUMAN TEST SUBJECT AND EARN $2,000

On opposite end of the spectrum, there are studies known as clinical trials that test new drugs on willing subjects. These have much greater risks than observational studies, but the rewards are far more lucrative.

I know this may be a little controversial—signing your body to gain some extra spending money. But when I decided to write this book, I wanted to find the best ways to generate extra income and realized this technique was well worth adding to the list. There aren't many other ways an individual can make $5,000 in a week, and sometimes the trial itself benefits the volunteer.

Before a new drug or treatment is available to the public, it must go through a rigorous process of clinical testing monitored by the FDA to see if the medication is ready for mass consumption. The testing phase is incredibly long, and most drugs that undergo preclinical testing never make it to human trials. The drugs that make it to human trials must first pass an evaluation process by the FDA. This pretrial evaluation scrutinizes everything from the way the trials are designed to the severity of side effects.

The stages of drug development are as follows:

Stage 1—Animals Tested: Before any drug can submitted for human trials, it must first be tested on laboratory animals to see if there are any negative side effects.

Stage 2—IND Application: The Investigational New Drug Application is reviewed by the FDA and local institutional review board to examine the results of the animal testing and to decide if the drug will continue with human trials. The board will review the protocols of the clinical trials, such as the type of people that may participate, the length of the study, dosage, etc., to see if the study is acceptable and will protect patients from harm.

Stage 3—Phase 1 Testing: This is the first stage of a clinical trial and is done in healthy volunteers to determine what side effects the drug has and how the drug is metabolized. This is the first of three phases in which volunteers can get paid for their service. Typically, the number of subjects ranges from 20–80. If the drug does not reveal unacceptable levels of toxicity, then Phase 2 trials may begin. It should be noted that Phase 1 trials are also the most risky, because researchers are simply attempting to identify side effects in healthy individuals.

Stage 4—Phase 2 Testing: Once the drug is seemed safe, Phase 2 trials begin to determine effectiveness. The drug is given to people with a certain disease or condition and is compared with a group receiving another treatment or placebo. Typically, the number of patients ranges from a few dozen up to 300. Safety and side effects continue to be monitored.

Stage 5—Phase 3 Testing: If Phase 2 showed signs of effective-ness, Phase 3 trials begin on a larger scale. Researchers collect more information on effectiveness and safety while testing dif-ferent dosages and in combination with other medications. The number of patients in this phase can range from a couple hundred to a few thousand people.

Stage 6—Review by Sponsor: Following the clinical trials, the drug is further studied by the sponsor company to gather more information on effectiveness and safety.

Stage 7—NDA Application & Review: The NDA, or New Drug Application, is the final and formal step to approve a new drug for marketing in the U.S. The NDA will include all results from animal and human trials and will be reviewed by the FDA. Depending on the results, the application will either be approved or denied.

The drug approval process normally takes several years, and it is the clini-cal trial portion that takes up most of the time. Remember, compensation in a clinical trial is a reward for risk. Because Phase 1 trials are the first trials in humans and testing for safety, they offer the most pay on average—around $2,000 per volunteer. The further along the trial you decide to volunteer, the less you are likely to receive. Once Phase 3 trials begin, the average payout is $400 and it becomes increasingly difficult to participate. If you don't have the specific disease the medication is used to treat, you are out of luck. However, this can be beneficial for an individual with a hard-to-treat condition. A Phase 3 trial might offer a better treatment option as well as the ability to get paid.

If you are interested in participating in clinical trials, check out the following website to see if any are in your area:

www.centerwatch.com/clinical-trials

I would like to remind you that participating in observational studies or clinical trials is not without risk. Speak with the researchers hosting the studies to determine any expected side effects and see if signing up is right for you. For most, simple observational studies are the least risky way to make a few hundred dollars. For those who are healthy and in good shape, a Phase 1 clinical trial might be a good way to bring in a couple thousand dollars.

Zach's Income Rating: Research Studies ★★★★☆ / Clinical Trials ★★☆☆☆

These two techniques score on different levels for various reasons. Research studies are generally simple and you can make a few dollars for only a couple minutes of your time. They don't pay as much as clinical trials, but they involve much less risk. Clinical trials should only be completed if you are in desperate need of income or have a specific disease that isn't being managed with previously approved medication. They pay more money, but since they are testing for side effects, there is also much greater risk.

III. SECRET INCOME STRATEGIES OF THE RICH AND SAVVY

This is the most investment-heavy section of the book. Here, you will find some of the best moneymaking secrets in America. Some opportunities require only a few dollars, while some require several thousand dollars to partake.

CHAPTER 16:

THE 1960'S TRICK THAT CAN "JUICE" YOUR DIVIDENDS FOR AN EXTRA $239,880

One of the most powerful tools to increase your wealth is a secret few investors know about.

In many cases, this strategy can be used to increase the value of your investments by 20% or more, just by a simple phone call or few clicks with your online broker. And as you'll see in a moment, that can mean tens or even hundreds of thousands of dollars for you.

Most people think there is only one way to own equity in a business, which is to buy shares through a broker, wait for the share price to increase and collect dividends along the way. The truth is there is a second way to hold and own these assets that can result in a completely different outcome for you as an investor.

Most stockbrokers don't want you to know about it because this cheap, simple and safe way to drastically increase your dividend payments doesn't require a brokerage account. In fact, shortly after this investing tool was created, Wall Street successfully persuaded Congress to forbid advertising to the general public because of its ability to shatter commissions for brokers and fund managers.

However, this simple trick has the power to multiply your invest-ments' value—and it only take a few minutes to complete. Let me show you how . . .

THE HISTORY OF THIS MONEY MULTIPLIER

The opportunity to partake in "dividend juicing" came about in the 1960s, when America was experiencing a period of rapid economic growth. Some refer to it as "the good old days"—when American industry prospered, the crime rate was low and we were undoubtedly the most powerful country in the world. It was a time when the interstate highways, schools, dams and bridges that we still use today were built—and it took a lot of man-power to get us there.

At that time, the few companies capable of handling big projects were in need of serious capital. In order to get the funding these companies needed, the government allowed this group of companies to sell shares of stock directly to the public rather than go through brokers and money managers. Now the average American could easily become an investor and start earning returns on their money just like the big guys on Wall Street.

Some of these companies gave huge discounts for buying shares directly through the company and encouraged investors by offering large dividend payouts that could be automatically reinvested in the company. Because of this, ordinary Americans could start off small, sometimes with as little as one share, and accumulate thousands of dollars without investing another penny.

But like I said, Wall Street lobbied Congress into passing a bill that made it illegal for these companies to advertise their programs to the public, so very few people utilize this strategy.

As *The Wall Street Journal* wrote:

> *"DRIPs are the best-kept secret on Wall Street,"* says Vita Nelson,
> editor of Moneypaper, a newsletter devoted to DRIPs.

Most people haven't heard about them for one simple reason—companies can't advertise their DRIPs. Why? Securities and Exchange Commission rules won't let them say much about this fabulous way of saving and building wealth, except to existing shareholders.

Or as Tim McAleenan Jr. of The Conservative Income Investor put it, it's:

The best-kept secret of the long-term dividend investor.

Historically, you had to directly contact the company in order to enroll in their program, but today, many online brokers will help reinvest your dividends for little to no cost—you'll just have to look at the fine print to make sure it is an option.

Now let's get into the details and show you how much these programs can make you . . .

UNLOCK THE POWER OF DRIPS

Today, more than 1,000 companies offer a way to invest with them directly through dividend reinvestment plans (DRIPs). To participate, most companies with DRIPs require that you own just one share. As I will show, these DRIPs allow you to "juice," or multiply, your dividends substantially.

You are probably aware that most companies pay out dividends to their investors on a quarterly basis. If you are enrolled in a DRIP policy, every time a dividend is paid, it is automatically reinvested into more shares of the company's stock. The next time a dividend is paid, you have more shares, which means your dividend payment continues to grow. The cycle continues, and before you know it, you're collecting five times more dividends than you were when you bought the stock without putting another penny into the investment.

When dividend gains are repeatedly reinvested into additional shares of a company, the power of compounding takes over. With compounding, you earn returns on your returns from prior periods. While the rate of return may be the same or vary year to year, since you reinvest the dividends, your investment balance grows exponentially. A small number of shares can grow into a large number over the long term, even without future purchases.

To show you how this dividend "juicing" works, let's take a closer look at an elite U.S. business that can boost your dividends by more than 250%: Annaly Capital Management (NYSE: NLY).

Here's how a hypothetical $10,000 NLY investment would look after reinvesting dividends in a DRIP for 20 years. For calculation purposes, we're assuming annual dividend growth of 4% and an annual stock price increase of 6%.

Note: These numbers are purely hypothetical for demonstration purposes.

With DRIP

Date	Shares	Price	Value	Dividend Per Share	Annual Income	Shares Bought
2018	1,000.00	10.00	10,000.00	0.30	300.00	28.30
2019	1,028.30	10.60	10,900.00	0.31	320.83	28.55
2020	1,056.86	11.24	11,874.83	0.32	342.93	28.79
2021	1,085.65	11.91	12,930.25	0.34	366.36	29.02
2022	1,114.67	12.62	14,072.43	0.35	391.20	29.23
2023	1,143.90	13.38	15,307.97	0.36	417.52	29.43
2024	1,173.33	14.19	16,643.97	0.38	445.39	29.62
2025	1,202.96	15.04	18,088.00	0.39	474.90	29.80
2026	1,232.75	15.94	19,648.18	0.41	506.13	29.96
2027	1,262.71	16.89	21,333.21	0.43	539.17	30.11
2028	1,292.82	17.91	23,152.37	0.44	574.11	30.24
2029	1,323.06	18.98	25,115.61	0.46	611.04	30.37
2030	1,353.43	20.12	27,233.59	0.48	650.06	30.48
2031	1,383.90	21.33	29,517.67	0.50	691.29	30.58
2032	1,414.48	22.61	31,980.02	0.52	734.83	30.66
2033	1,445.14	23.97	34,633.64	0.54	480.79	30.74
2034	1,475.88	25.40	37,492.25	0.56	829.29	30.80
2035	1,506.67	26.93	40,571.28	0.58	880.45	30.85
2036	1,537.52	28354	43,886.01	0.61	934.42	30.88
2037	1,568.40	30.26	47,453.59	0.63	991.32	30.91
2038	1,599.31	32.07	51,292.12	0.66	1,051.29	30.92

Without DRIP

Date	Shares	Price	Value	Dividend Per Share	Annual Income
2018	1,000.00	10.00	10,000.00	0.30	300.00
2019	1,000.00	10.60	10,900.00	0.31	312.00
2020	1,000.00	11.24	11,548.00	0.32	324.48
2021	1,000.00	11.91	12,234.64	0.34	337.46
2022	1,000.00	12.62	12,962.23	0.35	350.96
2023	1,000.00	13.38	13,733.21	0.36	365.00
2024	1,000.00	14.19	14,550.19	0.38	379.60
2025	1,000.00	15.04	15,415.90	0.39	394.78
2026	1,000.00	15.94	16,333.26	0.41	410.57
2027	1,000.00	16.89	17,305.36	0.43	426.99
2028	1,000.00	17.91	18,335.47	0.44	444.07
2029	1,000.00	18.98	19,427.06	0.46	461.84

Without DRIP *(continued)*

2030	1,000.00	20.12	20,583.80	0.48	480.31
2031	1,000.00	21.33	21,809.59	0.50	499.52
2032	1,000.00	22.61	23,108.59	0.52	519.50
2033	1,000.00	23.97	24,485.08	0.54	540.28
2034	1,000.00	25.40	25,943.80	0.56	561.89
2035	1,000.00	26.93	27,489.62	0.58	584.37
2036	1,000.00	28354	29,127.76	0.61	607.74
2037	1,000.00	30.26	30,863.74	0.63	632.05
2038	1,000.00	32.07	32,703.41	0.66	657.34

As you can see, you start with 1,000 shares. But as the stock pays dividends, you automatically buy more shares. By the end of 20 years, you own nearly 1,600 shares, without putting in an additional cent of your own cash.

Additionally, all of those shares continue to pay dividends. You go from collecting $300 a year to $1,051.29 as your position grows.

Notice what the compounding does to your total return. Again, assuming a modest growth rate of 6%, your $10,000 initial investment is worth $51,292 in just 20 years—well over five times your money, producing gains 81.9% larger than a regular stock purchase!

This is, of course, is just a hypothetical example. Why don't we take a look at a historical example that shows the value of this strategy? Consider your standard blue chip companies that have been around for decades, such as Exxon Mobil, McDonald's and Proctor & Gamble. These companies had an average rate of return of about 10% for the past 20 years—pretty standard for a quality company. Not spectacular, but not outrageously good, either. We will also include a couple companies that performed extremely well over that time frame, including TJX Companies and Nike:

Company	Initial investment	Total return without DRIP	Total return with DRIP	Difference with DRIP	Total gain juiced by...
Exxon Mobil	$10,000	$64,083	$79,791	$15,708	**24.5%**
McDonald's	$10,000	$74,744	$92,058	$17,314	**23.2%**
Proctor & Gamble	$10,000	$64,568	$78,463	$13,895	**21.5%**
TJ Maxx	$10,000	$868,465	$1,016,200	$147,735	**17.0%**
Nike	$10,000	$222,049	$267,277	$45,228	**20.4%**
Total	*$10,000*	*$1,293,909*	*$1,533,789*	*$239,880*	**18.5%**

As you can see, the dividend reinvestment strategy significantly increased the total return on the investment. By *not* reinvesting dividends, shareholders *lost* between $13,895 and $147,735 worth of value.

When you look at those numbers, there is no question about how valuable dividend reinvesting can be for your portfolio. If you invested $10,000 in TJX in 1995, you would be sitting on $868,465, or a cool $1,016,200 if you had reinvested dividends, a difference of $147,735. It's an astonishing figure. However, there are more benefits to a DRIP than meets the eye.

MAKE THE MOST OF YOUR MONEY

Besides utilizing the power of compounding, DRIPs provide a number of additional advantages. When you purchase shares of a company through a broker, you're hit with a brokerage fee. Over time, these fees can take a huge bite out of your returns. DRIPs allow you to reinvest dividends back into the company without paying a brokerage fee. This can make a huge difference in your long-term returns. Once you've purchased at least one share of stock and enrolled in a DRIP, you'll be able to purchase partial shares of the company with your dividends. You won't have to save cash to purchase full shares.

Because you're investing in a DRIP periodically—usually quarterly, when dividends are paid—you're able to buy more shares of stock when the stock price is low and fewer shares of stock when its stock price is high. This is known as dollar cost averaging. This helps lower your overall purchase price of a stock, thereby boosting your returns.

While dividends are reported as capital gains, dividend reinvestment plans do not make any cash payouts. While stock prices may rise, no capital gains tax need be paid until the stock is sold. The longer the shares are held, the lower the tax rate. The lower your tax rate, the more gains you keep.

START "JUICING" YOUR DIVIDENDS TODAY

Today, over 1,000 companies offer DRIPs you can enroll in. Traditionally, you had to call the company directly in order to purchase shares, but now most online brokers such as Charles Schwab or Merrill Lynch offer the option to reinvest dividends at no cost. Remember, the sooner you start a DRIP, the sooner you'll enjoy magnified dividends, so start investing today to see the best results—it could mean the difference of $100k for your retirement.

Zach's Income Rating: ★★★★★

The best kept secret on Wall Street easily receives a five star rating. All it takes is a few minutes for you to increase your returns by 20% or more. Best of all, you only need a few dollars to get started—and this technique will significantly increase your wealth over time.

CHAPTER 17:

THE SECRET MARKET TRANSACTION THAT GENERATES $1,500 (OR MORE) IN INSTANT INCOME MONTH AFTER MONTH

If you don't plan on working for the rest of your life, you've probably looked for other ways to build retirement income. For instance, you probably have a savings account or maybe some certificates of deposit at a well-known bank. But these days, the payouts are so small and build so slowly that you almost shouldn't bother.

Maybe you own some precious metals or some nice real estate that you plan to sell. The downside is you can't count on them to provide the income you need when you need it. So hopefully, you've been a bit more ambitious, putting your money into stocks and bonds that pay nice dividends. All you need to do is sit back and watch the checks roll in. It's a great strategy, but it's also a little passive. Your money comes regularly, but on someone else's schedule.

That's why I recommend you complement your income strategy with one simple financial transaction. This little-known way of making money lets you boost your portfolio's payouts almost anytime you want without waiting for dividend checks to come in. Better still, if you use this strategy correctly, you can keep these instant payouts rolling in for as long as you want—adding more money to your account again and again.

You can use the money to buy gold or pay for groceries or any other life expenses immediately. It truly is cash when you want it.

Most people don't know about this loophole, because at its heart is something many investors don't understand—stock options.

MAKING MONEY WITH OPTIONS

There are many reasons stock options have a bad reputation. For one thing, if you don't have a financial degree, the terminology can be intimidating. They can sound complicated, too, with myriad "strike prices" to consider and "expiration dates" to keep track of. Then there are the scare stories about how risky options can be . . . and how a frighteningly large number of stock options "expire worthless." Who wants to invest in something that regularly loses all its value?

To be honest, I think a lot of brokers and analysts make options seem worse than they are to keep people away. It's not just greed or elitism, though. The truth is it is very easy for novice options investors to get in trouble and in way over their heads—and I wouldn't blame brokers for steering folks away from trouble.

If used properly, however, stock options can instantly deliver extra cash to your portfolio almost on demand, with very little work or even risk on your part. And as you'll see, they aren't too hard to understand or even profit from. For one thing, stock options trade alongside stocks on the major exchanges. You buy and sell them just like you do any stock. And like stocks, their prices go up and down in response to market conditions.

The biggest difference between stock trading and options trading is what you're trading. Stocks, of course, represent part ownership in a company. When you buy a stock, you buy a part of the company. When you sell your stock, you give up that ownership.

Options are a little more complicated. When you buy a stock option, you are actually buying rights to 100 shares of a given stock. Those rights expire at a given time, the expiration date, which is an integral part of every option sold.

You can pay money for the right to buy the 100 shares of stock at a set price—the strike price—before the option expires. That's called a call option.

Or you can pay money for the right to sell 100 shares of stock at the strike price before the option expires.

That's called a put option.

OPTIONS IN ACTION

Here's the thing . . .

Nowadays, when most people buy options, they are simply betting on short-term stock moves. Instead of buying shares of Wal-Mart, for example, these traders are buying options to bet on which way Wal-Mart's stock will move. If they think the price of Wal-Mart will go up, they buy calls. If they think the price of Wal-Mart will drop, they buy puts.

That's all well and good, but at the heart of the matter, these traders are gambling. You see, 76.5% of all options expire worthless, meaning these up and down bets rarely pay off for the gamblers. Frankly, it's not too far off to say that buying calls and puts is similar to buying a lotto ticket at the local gas station. No wonder the options market gets such a risky reputation.

The thing is our strategy is all about making money, not paying it. To do that, we take the other side of the trade—by selling the puts and the calls to those gamblers. With limited risk, no less.

THE OTHER SIDE ALWAYS GETS PAID

You see, when you buy an option, you are buying certain rights to the stock. However, just as with stocks, there are two sides to every trade. To buy a stock, someone has to sell it to you, and the same is true with options. For every options buyer, there must be an options seller. The difference is that instead of selling you their ownership in a company, an option seller is selling a commitment to honor the options contract.

The best opportunity is to sell put options. When you sell a put, you receive money in exchange for the obligation to buy the underlying stock at a set price. And when you sell a call, you get money in exchange for the obligation to sell the underlying stock at the strike price. It's called "writing options," and it's a lot less complicated than it sounds.

You may need special permission from your broker to make these kinds of trades. Most brokers consider this "Level I" or "Level II" trading, while other brokers call them "tiers." There's typically a standard three-page disclosure form to fill out, but don't let the hoops scare you.

In reality, this is some of the safest options trading you can do. You'll always be fully in control of the risks, and you just need to take some simple steps to stay out of trouble. In fact, if done correctly, it's no more risky than buying a stock outright.

Confused? Let's look at a simple analogy . . .

Suppose you're interested in buying a car that a dealership has listed on sale for $25,000. You love the car, but even the sale price is too high. You would much rather buy the vehicle for $20,000. So you walk into the shiny dealership showroom and tell the dealer that you're only willing to pay $20,000 for the car. You tell the dealer that if the car goes on sale for $20,000 in the next month, you'll buy it.

Then the dealer says "Deal!" opens his register and PAYS YOU $500 cash to leave your offer on the table for one month. You literally walk out of the dealership with $500 CASH and a chance at buying the car you like for $20,000.

Two things can happen from this point. Maybe you get a call in a few weeks and the dealer takes you up on your offer. You get a great deal on a car that you wanted to buy. Plus, you still get to keep your $500.

Or maybe you don't get a call from the dealer. A month passes, the dealer sells the car to someone else and you still get to keep your $500.

Not a bad deal, right? Well that's exactly how "put selling" works. But instead of offering to buy a car off the lot at a discount price, we're offering to buy shares of stock at a discount price. Let's take a look at another example.

Say you are looking to pick up shares in Microsoft. They are going for $50 a share, but you'd really like to pay a bit less than that. So you could write (sell) a put option on Microsoft with a strike price of $48 and an expiration date a few months into the future.

Technically, you are creating a contract and offering it up for sale, but don't sweat the details. Options contracts are standardized. All you need to tell your broker is that you want to "sell to open" a Microsoft $48 put option and they'll know what you mean. Your broker will enter your trade into the market, where you'll be randomly paired with someone looking to buy a Microsoft $48 put option. Whoever buys it will pay the current market price for the option, let's say $100—and that money (the premium) goes directly into your account.

That's instant income! And it's yours to keep, no matter what. Just like in our car buying example above.

Keep in mind that you sold an obligation to buy 100 shares of Microsoft at $48. If the share price dips below $48, the option buyer might exercise their rights and force you to buy. In that case, you'll want to set aside enough money to buy the shares if they end up dropping below the strike price. The formula is always 100 times the option's strike price for every option you sell—in this case, $4,800. It's called a cash-secured put, and it means you'll never be caught by surprise.

(You can also limit how much you'll have to pay out of pocket by establishing a margin account with your broker. It allows you to pay just a portion of the stock price while your broker loans you the rest of the money to cover the cost.)

Once you've sold your put and have cash set aside, all you do is wait. Remember, someone holding a put won't exercise it if the stock's price is above the option's strike price. Why sell a stock for less than you can get on the open market?

Once you're an options writer, you don't have to worry about buying the stock unless the current price is below the strike price. In our Microsoft example, you wouldn't have to buy shares unless they fell below the $48 strike price. If the stock stayed above $48 up until the option expired, you'd never have to buy the stock. Instead, the option would expire worthless and you would get to keep the premium.

Now, if shares of Microsoft fell below $48, then the option might get exercised and you'd have to buy 100 shares of the stock for $48 apiece.

Luckily, you'd have that cash standing by. Your broker can handle everything automatically.

And that's how you get instant income. By selling cash-secured puts, you can buy shares of companies you want to own at prices you get to decide. If the company is trading too high, sell a cash-secured put to make income until the company is within your price range. For more information, contact your broker and find out if this income-generating technique is right for you.

Of course, if the option in our example were exercised, you'd be holding 100 shares of Microsoft. So what to do? How about collecting some extra income by selling some calls against it? That's what we'll talk about in Chapter 18.

Editor's note: Remember, options involve risk. Please make sure you know the risks or contact your financial adviser before you buy or sell options.

Zach's Income Rating: ★★★★★

Put selling receives five stars because of its effectiveness in generating instant, useable income. No other strategy allows you to buy stocks at the price you want to pay while giving you an instant premium to do so. The only caveat is that this strategy may require a minimum amount of cash in order to be approved by your broker, usually ranging from $5,000–20,000 in "investable" cash.

P.S. LEVERAGE YOUR GOLD PORTFOLIO WITH OPTION SELLING

One of the best ways to invest in gold or precious metal miners is through put selling. Since the industry is cyclical, selling put options will allow you to acquire shares of companies that you want to own for less than you would want to pay. Best of all, you can keep the premiums to purchase bullion outright.

CHAPTER 18:

GET AN ADDITIONAL 2% CONTRIBUTION MATCH FROM YOUR BROKER ON YOUR 401(K)

In this chapter, I will reveal one of the best ways to increase returns on your portfolio without purchasing any additional shares of stock or leveraging your positions with risky speculations. In fact, it's fast, easy, and a low risk way to earn an extra 2% bonus on companies you already own—all done through your broker. It's so low risk that you should be able to use this strategy in your IRA and 401(k).

The strategy I am talking about is called writing covered calls (or sometimes "buy-write"), and mastering it is simply a matter of understanding what you're getting into. Just like writing puts (which we discussed in Chapter 17), this strategy for generating income on stocks you own is through an options strategy.

CALLING MORE INCOME

When you sell (write) a call option, you agree to sell a stock at the option's strike price—but only if the stock price is above the strike price. Again, there's a time limit for this to happen, and you are paid a premium you get to keep.

Let's say you own 100 shares of Microsoft and, for the sake of example, MSFT is trading at $50 a share. The stock pays a quarterly dividend of 31 cents a share.

That's not bad . . . but you could consider boosting your payouts from Microsoft by selling calls options against your shares. Let's say you decide to sell an MSFT call option with a strike price of $57.50 that expires in four months. To do that, you'd tell your broker you want to "sell to open" a Microsoft June $57.50 call option. (Note: This is just an example, not an actual recommendation.)

Your broker will essentially create a call options contract for you. Then he will sell the contract on the open market, where you'll be randomly paired with someone looking to buy a Microsoft June $57.50 call option. Whoever buys it will pay the current market price for the option. Let's say the going price is $175. Once the sale goes through, that $175 (the premium) will go directly into your account.

That's instant income!

Now, keep in mind you're on the hook to sell 100 shares of Microsoft to the call buyer if he exercises his rights. But with a strike price of $57.50, the buyer will exercise his rights only if shares trade above $57.50. If shares of MSFT don't trade above $57.50, the option will never be exercised. When it expires, you get to keep your shares PLUS the premium you received for selling the call option. You also get to collect any dividends Microsoft pays out while you're holding the stock.

In other words, you're effortlessly collecting "bonus" income with very little work. And that's not the end of it . . . because when the calls expire, you can collect more payouts by writing new calls against the stock. But what if the shares go above $57.50 and the call is exercised? No sweat!

Say Microsoft goes to $58 a share and the call is exercised. You're already holding 100 shares of stock, so your call is covered. It is, in fact, a covered call. Your broker will automatically sell the shares from your account. You'll be paid $57.50 a share, and you'll also get to keep the premium you received for selling the call in the first place—not to mention all the dividends you collected the entire time you held the shares.

Without lifting a finger, you've collected a respectable profit.

Of course, the downside is that you no longer own the Microsoft shares. You'll miss out on future dividend payments, not to mention any capital gains if the stock continues trading higher. That's why I suggest strongly adhering to three rules before you use a covered call strategy.

THREE RULES FOR WRITING CALLS FOR INCOME

First, you MUST own shares of the stock you write calls on—100 shares of stock for every call contract you want to sell. Imagine writing a $57.50 call on Microsoft but not owning any shares. If they're called away, you'll need to buy them on the open market at whatever price they happen to be. If they're selling for $60 . . . guess what? You'll have to buy 100 shares for $60 each and then sell them for $57.50. If you already own the shares, it won't really matter what the going market price is.

Second, write calls only against stocks that you are able and willing to part with. In other words, sell calls fully expecting them to be exercised. If you'll miss the shares for any reason, don't risk having them called away.

Third, make sure that you pick an attractive strike price—the agreed-upon price that you will sell your stock for if the owner of the call contract decides to "exercise" his right to buy shares from you. Since you can pick any strike price, make sure you pick one that gives you a fair price for your stock. If you'd be unhappy selling your Microsoft shares for $57.50 each, don't sell calls with a $57.50 strike price.

THREE RULES FOR WRITING CALLS FOR INCOME

1. Don't write calls on stocks you don't already own. Write one call option for every 100 shares of stock you own.
2. Only write call contracts against stocks that you are willing to sell. Do not write calls against your stock position if you are unable or unwilling to part with your stock.
3. Choose a strike price that you will be satisfied with if you are required to sell your stock. If the call contracts are "exercised," you will sell at an agreed-upon price—make sure it's a price you find attractive.

If you're prepared to follow these rules, you'll find that selling calls against your stocks is an easy and relatively safe way to boost your portfolio's income. However, before you start writing options, there are a few steps you may need to take.

HOW TO START TRADING

As I said earlier, you should be able to sell call options right from your current brokerage account. Depending on the broker, you might even be able to sell covered calls in your IRA, but there is a chance you may need to ask your broker for permission to make options trades.

Brokers have an obligation to make sure their clients don't get in over their heads. They won't let you trade options if they think you are too inexperienced. That's why clients must meet certain requirements before they're allowed to start trading options.

To simplify the process, brokers often break types of options trades into "levels" or "tiers." In general, the higher the level or tier, the more risky the activity. However, levels and tiers are not universal—brokers set their own standards and criteria for each. What one broker considers a "Level 1" trade might be a "Level 2" trade at another broker.

Luckily, writing covered calls is considered very low risk (because it is), so it should be fairly easy for you to get permission. Simply look on your broker's website for options trading, fill out the required forms for permission to sell covered calls and then wait for your broker's approval. After that, it's merely a matter of finding the option you want to sell.

Look for a button on your broker's web page to trade options, enter the stock symbol and then look for an "option chain" or a way to manually enter the expiration and the strike price. When in doubt, call your broker to figure out where to find the option you want to sell. Just remember to follow the rules I set out for you and you'll be 100% in control of any risks.

Before you know it, you may soon find yourself creating perpetual income. You'll buy shares of stock and then collect extra income by selling calls against your shares. If the calls expire worthless, you'll sell new calls—collecting even more bonus income. And if the calls are exercised, you'll earn a nice profit on your position. Use this trick to earn income from stocks that don't pay dividends . . . or to increase the money you receive from your favorite dividend-paying stocks.

Editor's note: Remember, options involve risk. Please make sure you know the risks or contact your financial adviser before you buy or sell options.

Zach's Income Rating: ★★★★★

Selling covered calls is one of the best ways to earn income through the stock market. You earn instant cash while choosing a price at which you wish to sell shares of stock you own. Using this strategy, you can earn hundreds, if not thousands of dollars a month. The only caveat is that you must own at least 100 shares of the stock to sell covered calls, which would require an initial investment.

CHAPTER 19:

THE DIVIDEND GUARANTEED BY LAW ACCORDING TO THE TRUST INDENTURE ACT OF 1939

As an income investor, the last thing you want to see flashing on the news screen is "More U.S. companies are cutting their dividends amid financial woes . . . " Pretty soon, your portfolio is generating significantly less income and you are left wondering how to make up the difference.

What if I told you there is a way to guarantee your dividends by law, and it doesn't involve any tricky loopholes or lawyers and legal counsels? In fact, there is a fairly common type of security that guarantees dividends and can sometimes yield more than stocks themselves. I'm talking about a security most investors are hesitant to touch but, after I explain in a moment, you should have no fear of getting into this market.

These tricky securities I am referring to are **corporate bonds**.

Corporate bonds are debt instruments issued by corporations looking to raise money for various projects. The corporate bond market is enormous, too . . . valued at over $9.5 trillion. Many companies have bonds that trade on secondary markets after they are initially sold—from large companies like General Electric and Apple to Exxon and Harrah's Entertainment, companies from every sector use bonds to raise capital.

Here's the secret: **Purchasing corporate bonds can be as easy as buying stock**. You don't hear about bonds as much as you hear about the movement of stocks, but corporate bonds can be very liquid and extremely profitable and should be included in any diversified portfolio.

As I said, most people are hesitant to touch bonds. It might be due to inexperience or because they were taught bonds yield significantly less than stocks. If you fall in either of these two categories, let me give you the rundown on the basics.

When bonds are first auctioned by companies, they are typically sold for $1,000, which is known as the "par value." Most of these bonds will include a semiannual "coupon" payment, which is equivalent to a dividend. These payments will vary, with riskier bonds offering more attractive yields. The bond also has a set time frame, or maturity date, when the par value will be paid back to the investor. So as a bond investor, you receive all of the coupon payments plus the par value at the maturity date.

Once the bond is auctioned, it can be sold on the secondary securities market and traded between investors like you and me. Depending on how well the company performs, the bond can rise or drop in value, just like a stock. The thing is, your coupon payments will remain the same even if the bond drops in value, and you will still receive the same par value when the bond matures. For example, if the bond has a yearly coupon payment of 9%, or $90 a year, at its initial auction, that coupon payment will remain the same even if the bond drops in price to $750 (or any other price). So if you buy the bond at a discount, you get a greater yield.

The SEC says (emphases ours):

> If the company runs into financial difficulties, **it still has a legal obligation to make timely payments of interest and principal**. The company has no similar obligation to pay dividends to shareholders. **In a bankruptcy, bond investors have priority over shareholders in claims on the company's assets.**

Thus, bonds are contracts guaranteed by law, and that includes their coupon payments. Even if a CEO of a company declares a dividend cut, your coupon payments are still guaranteed. The only way you would not receive your payment is if the company goes bankrupt. In the case of bankruptcy, bonds are often tied to the company's physical assets, which are sold off to pay creditors—and that's you, the bondholder. So while common stockholders are at the end of the line and rarely collect payment on a bankruptcy, bondholders are at the front and will often collect proceeds from the sale of assets.

While it's best to avoid bankruptcy altogether, it's not the worst-case scenario for secured bondholders. But if you are looking for safety, how can you tell which bonds are right for you?

Just like any other security, corporate bonds can either be high grade or high yield. Usually, the higher the yield, the higher the risk of a company not being able to pay off their debt. High-grade, or investment-grade, bonds are rated AAA+ through BBB-. These bonds are issued by the companies with the best credit that have the lowest chance of defaulting on their debt.

High-yield, or speculative, bonds range from BB to anything below. These bonds offer higher yields and are often discounted compared with their investment-grade counterparts. While a high-grade bond from Apple might yield 3%, a speculative bond from a distressed energy company could yield over 100% returns—better than most stocks—while paying a guaranteed coupon.

Here are a few examples of bonds expiring in 20 or more years that can bring you a solid stream of income for years down the road. These bonds are sold by some of the biggest and safest companies in the world, which is why they are priced with a premium. But over the 20 years you hold the bond, you will more than make up for the premium and have a continual flow of income each year. To locate the bond with your broker, simply enter the CUSIP and the information should be readily available.

Microsoft	08/08/46
Yield	3.7%
Price	$102.332
CUSIP	594918BT0
Rating	AA+

Johnson & Johnson	08/15/37
Yield	5.95%
Price	$136.24
CUSIP	478160AN4
Rating	AAA

Exxon	03/01/46
Yield	4.114%
Price	$109.84
CUSIP	30231GAW2
Rating	AA+

To generate higher income payments, consider high-yield bonds priced at a discount. Keep in mind high-yield bonds have enticing returns because the companies that issue them have less-than-perfect credit scores. While it is not certain they will default on their payment, there is a higher chance they might not be able to pay. The old adage "High risk, high reward" certainly holds true when it comes to corporate bonds. I must also note, however, that most high-yield bonds end up paying their coupons and principal. In fact, over 96% of high-yield bonds make payment without default. So how much risk is too much? It is up to the investor to decide.

Corporate bonds are a great way to get a guaranteed income stream and diversify your portfolio against unsystematic risk. Remember, even if a company goes bankrupt, bondholders often receive a percentage of the par value, because bonds tend to be secured to assets that can be sold off during bankruptcy. Bonds are not as complicated as many people think—simply call your broker or check online to see what your options are. Many investors have made a fortune on bonds, so don't let bonds' boring reputation discourage your profits.

Zach's Income Rating: ★★★★★

Corporate bonds should be an integral part of everyone's retirement portfolio. They offer income payments on a fixed schedule that can be used to plan for major life events such as weddings or tuition payments for a child. They are also contracts that are guaranteed by law, which makes them some of the safest investments around. Fixed payments, safety guaranteed by law, and high returns are hard to pass up!

CHAPTER 20:

HOW TO GET A SEMI-ANNUAL CHECK FROM YOUR LOCAL WATERWORKS DIVISION

Every month, you pay taxes to fund schools, maintain bridges and support your local water supply. These bills can certainly be annoying . . . After all, it seems like the government rarely uses your money to benefit the local economy. With potholed streets and tainted water lines, it makes you wonder why we even pay taxes.

Unbeknownst to the average American, there is a way to have these public works pay you a semiannual check, and few take advantage of this lucrative investing strategy. It is a type of investing that predates Colonial America—you can find examples dating all the way back to the Renaissance!

I am talking about **municipal bonds**, which are some of the safest ways to generate income from your local public works. Currently, the municipal bond market is worth $3.7 trillion, and this includes issuers from a multitude of areas. Schools, transportation, waterworks, the lottery, airports, utilities and power plants, you name it—these bonds help support the construction and maintenance of our infrastructure and economy.

Municipal bonds typically have much-lower yields than corporate bonds, paying 1–3% for the length of issue. However, that range extends, depending on the type of bond and the credit rating of issuer. The reason for the lower returns is the increased level of safety coming from government guarantees.

Higher-yield municipal bonds generally come with more risk to the buyer, but there is one reason I am a fan of these high-yield munis. The default rate on municipal bonds is extremely low. In 2014, not one municipal bond rated by Moody's defaulted. From 1970–2014, only 95 municipal bonds defaulted out of the trillions of dollars' worth in the markets. So even for the high-risk municipal bonds, your chance of getting paid is extremely high. This makes municipal bonds some of the safest investments, behind U.S. Treasury bonds.

Municipal bonds come in two forms: general obligation and revenue yield.

1. With a **general obligation bond**, the issuer pays back the coupon and principal based on a scheduled time frame, just like a typical corporate bond. They are secured by the issuer and usually voted on.

2. A **revenue bond** is a little different. The principal and coupon on these bonds are paid by the revenues derived from tolls and fees from the proceeds of the bond issue. Highway tolls, water bills, subsidized housing and other operating incomes are examples of revenue streams generated for these types of municipal bonds. Just think . . . every time you pass through a tollbooth, you are likely generating revenue for a bondholder . . . and that bondholder could be you.

Municipal bonds usually come in $5,000 denominations—a bit pricier than corporate bonds but still affordable for the mature investor. Why not take advantage and have public works pay you for a change? With an extremely low default rate, your investment is practically guaranteed.

Another special feature of most municipal bonds is that they provide tax-except income. Normally, when you receive payments from income-generating assets such as dividend-paying stocks or corporate bonds, the income is taxable. Because of municipal bonds' unique provisions, you can generate income tax-free. This includes both state and federal taxes.

(However, there is a small caveat. Before you purchase a municipal bond, you should be aware that most, but not all, municipal bonds are tax-free. So depending on the state or county issuing the bond, a bond-holder may be liable for state or even federal taxes, but this is rare.)

Municipal bonds are a great way to have your local government pay you for a change—tax-free. With an extremely low default rate, even risky municipal bonds have almost guaranteed payouts, so take advantage today.

Contact your financial adviser or broker to get more information on which municipal bonds are right for you. A typical online broker such as Fidelity or Merrill Lynch will have options to purchase municipal bonds.

Zach's Income Rating: ★★★★☆

Municipal bonds are a great way to have your local public works supply you with a steady stream of income. Municipals bonds have some of the highest credit ratings, but this in turn brings down their returns. For that reason, municipal bonds earn a four star rating.

CHAPTER 21:

EARN AN 8% RETURN ON YOUR MONEY . . . AS A MODERN-DAY LOAN SHARK

On a cold winter morning, you wake up to a loud knock on the front door. Immediately, your heart sinks . . .

"Open up, Sonny!" says a familiar voice with a harsh Brooklyn accent. "I know you're in there!"

You look out the window and see two black vans surrounded by six hulking figures standing still by the end of the driveway. There is nowhere to run, nowhere to hide . . . For months, you have been avoiding this man, and you now must answer the door to accept the inevitable.

As you stand up and slowly walk across the room, you think back on what went wrong and why you chose to take a loan at a 30% interest rate to cover the cost of your mortgage when you were on the brink of default.

You turn the key, and the door flies open before you can even reach the handle. A towering man takes up the entire doorframe and barges in without hesitation. What happens next haunts you for decades . . .

It's unfortunate how desperate times used to call for desperate measures. If someone was in a short-term bind for cash, one of the only ways of gaining access to capital was through a loan shark, who often charged exorbitant interest rates paired with violent tactics for those who were not able to make payments on time.

Today, people are still in need of loans that banks won't provide. Whether it is refinancing credit cards, putting an addition on a house or a simple need for cash, you can become a "loan shark" without the tactics or stigma of the past.

With the onset of the technological era, financing has become easier, and borrowers have more options when it comes to securing cash in times of distress. In fact, it is through new technologies that you can become the modern-day loan shark (without the early-morning shakedowns and entourage, of course). Let me show you how . . .

For those who want to refinance or take out a loan that banks will not provide, there are special apps and programs that will connect potential borrowers with willing lenders. These "peer to peer" lending programs allow financing through contributions from individual investors.

Instead of going to a bank, the borrower uses a peer-to-peer lending program, most likely a website or mobile app. The analysts working for the website will look at the potential borrower's credit, income and debt to see if they qualify for a loan. If they are approved, their loan can be filled by ordinary investors—people like you and me.

Of all the peer-to-peer lending programs, there is one platform in particular that brings in consistent and lucrative returns for investors. They have a rigorous screening process for borrowers that approves only 10% of potential loans. This ensures that only the most responsible and qualified candidates take out loans—and therefore are most likely to pay them back.

The incentives to lend in this program are pretty high. The interest charged on loans usually ranges from 7–30%, depending on the borrower's credit score. The annualized returns from these loans normally fluctuates between 5–9% a year. By cutting out the bank as the middleman, the borrower can secure a loan that might otherwise be denied, and the investor can earn more than 20 times the interest of the average savings account.

Another great aspect of this program is you don't have to support a loan in its entirety. Rather, you can put as little as $25 into multiple loans, into as many different tranches as you like. That means if one person is asking for a $10,000 loan to refinance their credit card and another is asking for a $4,000 personal loan, you can put in $25 into the first and $25 in the other.

You can, of course, invest much larger sums if you wish. Many investors invest in a basket of loans across various tranches, or credit scores, in order to hedge their risk with higher-grade loans while attempting to capture gains associated with riskier loans. Loans typically come in either 36-month or 60-month terms, and you will receive monthly payments based off of the principal and interest earned—it's that easy.

The platform I am speaking of is called Lending Club, which is one of the best peer-to-peer lending programs around. Since 2009, Lending Club has issued close to $16 billion in loans. Their loans range in grade from A–G, with A-grade borrowers having best credit scores and likelihood of repayment and G-grade borrowers having the highest likelihood of default. To demonstrate the difference, an A-grade loan has an average interest rate of 7.58%, while a G-grade loan has an average interest rate of 23.9%. Check out the graphic on different loan grades below:

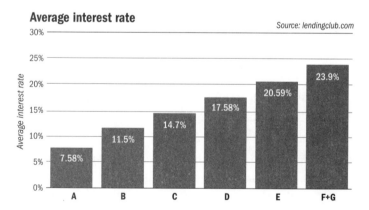

What loans you invest in is up to you—just remember that higher yield entails higher risk. For example, from 2007–2015, F- and G-rated bonds only had an 8.02% annualized return, even though the interest rate was close to 24%. If you invest in a basket of loans across multiple tranches, your annualized return should still be around 8%, with a 99.9% chance of positive returns.

The key to success is to spread your money across a variety of loans. If one person fails to make a payment, it won't adversely affect you if you manage to properly diversify. Lending Club loans have a default rate of 4%, so that means four out of every 100 borrowers fail to make their payments. Typically, defaults are associated with lower-grade loans, so if you diversify properly, the odds are in your favor.

For example, the historical returns by grade are shown below:

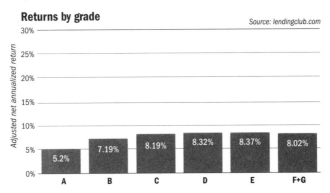

Even though the lower-grade loans have higher interest rates, their historical returns are significantly less than their interest rates because the default rate is greater.

Although Lending Club is the biggest peer-to-peer lender out there, there are a number of other programs that connect borrowers with willing lenders. Take Prosper, for example. This peer-to-peer lending site has issued over $6 billion in loans since 2006 and offers very similar terms to Lending Club. Their loans come in 36- or 60-month terms, with an annualized return of 7.5%. These peer-to-peer programs are virtually identical when it comes to investing, so which program is chosen is up to the individual investor.

If you check out the image below, you will see that Prosper claims to have higher estimated returns compared with Lending Club:

Estimated returns using Prosper

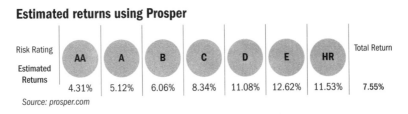

According to Prosper, that's what your estimated returns could look like, after accounting for defaults and fees. This is different than looking at historical returns, which is what Lending Club shows to potential investors. This is important to keep in mind when selecting a program to invest in.

Either way, both platforms offer a great way to get started in the peer-to-peer lending sphere.

With peer-to-peer lending, you're like a modern-day loan shark! When people want to refinance or take out a loan that banks won't approve, borrowers can seek out individual lenders like you and me to supply the cash. It's a highly lucrative way to make money in any market condition. With close to $16 billion in loans issued, Lending Club is one of the largest platforms to get started in the peer-to-peer lending industry. If Lending Club isn't your style, go for Prosper, which offers more specialized loans and higher estimated returns.

If you are hesitant to start, check out www.lendingclub.com or www.prosper.com for more information. Their websites provide a plethora of information that will help you make the right decision.

Editor's Note: We have no affiliation to Lending Club, Prosper or their subsidiaries.

Zach's Income Rating: ★★★★☆

Peer-to-peer sharing is a great way earn close to an 8% interest rate on your investment. This technique is great way to build up a portfolio because you can start for as little as $25 dollars. Some loans are riskier than others, so make sure to spread your money across a basket of different ratings to balance your portfolio. Risk factors in certain bond categories make these investments a four star opportunity.

CHAPTER 22:

NEVER LOSE A PENNY WITH THESE CRASH-PROOF INVESTMENTS

When people think of risk-free, safe investments, they typically think of Treasury bonds, savings accounts and certificates of deposit. While these accounts are "safe" by the standard definition, they offer almost no return on your investment.

In the past, these investments were a solid choice for almost any portfolio. In some years, Treasury bonds yielded close to 15%. Unfortunately, times have changed. Safe investments no longer yield anything of value—most return less than 1% a year and thus can't even keep up with inflation. Investors must now take on more risk to maintain the returns that were generated with less risk in years past.

There are a few instruments in the depths of the financial world, however, that provide the ability to generate sizable returns while risking almost nothing on your original investment. Worst case, your account may never grow, but best case, you could see returns up to 70% at near zero risk. Let's take a look.

EVERBANK MARKETSAFE CDS

Based out of Jacksonville, Florida, this little-known bank is not only the sponsor of the Jacksonville Jaguars, but offers an investment that is guaranteed to never lose value.

The EverBank MarketSafe CD is a financial instrument that not many investors are familiar with. These little-known CDs are auctioned off by EverBank throughout the year and give investors the chance to earn up to 70% returns on their investment while having 100% principal protection. With the EverBank MarketSafe CD (as the name implies), you can invest knowing you won't lose a dime on your money while capturing significant upside depending on the performance of the underlying asset.

The CDs that EverBank auctions are based on a variety of factors—from BRICS performance to precious metals, commodities, currencies or even Japanese real estate. Typically, you must invest a minimum of $1,500 for five years. This means your money is going to be tied up, but with the benefit of receiving principal protection on your original investment.

Let's take a look at EverBank's recent auction of the MarketSafe Commodity Solutions CD, which bases its returns on the performance of WTI crude, gold, silver, soybeans, corn, sugar, copper and nickel. The way the CD works is that it takes the average return for the commodities each year and applies it to the principal at the end of the year. Because the CD is principal protected, even if the commodities lose value over the next five years, you are still guaranteed your original investment.

When the CD was issued, EverBank recorded the initial prices for each commodity. For the next five years on an annual predetermined pricing date, EverBank will record the prices of oil, gold, silver, soybeans, corn, sugar, copper and nickel. The new prices will be compared with the initial prices for each of these components. EverBank will keep track of the advance or decline for each component compared with the initial value.

In this example the potential gain for each component is subject to a 70% cap at each annual pricing for each component. At the end of the five years, EverBank will take an average of each of the five annual readings for each of the components. If the commodities are trading higher at maturity, you'll get your deposited principal back and paid a return based on the weighted average gain of these readings—up to a maximum return of 70%. If, for some reason, this weighted average is not positive, you're still guaranteed to get your deposited principal back at maturity. Additionally, because EverBank is a member of the FDIC, your investment is federally insured up to $250,000.

EverBank MarketSafe CDs are a great way to invest in various markets with extremely low risk. Check out EverBank's website (www.everbank.com) to find details regarding their next auction or more information on how MarketSafe CDs are guaranteed.

These opportunities only present themselves a few times a year, so don't delay in finding out more.

Zach's Income Rating: ★★★★★

Everbank CDs aren't well known, but they are one of the best investments around. Where else can you find a principal protected security that gives exposure to volatile markets such as oil and precious metals? For these reasons, Everbank CDs receive a five star rating.

SUPERCHARGED ANNUITIES, WITH FULL PRINCIPAL PROTECTION

Annuities have a bad rep in the investing world—and for good reason. Many people have lost money with variable annuities that are tied to the stock market, and fixed annuities have eroded returns with the inability to keep up with inflation.

However, there is one type of annuity that is better than the rest—and actually does investors a favor. These annuities offer the chance to make money in the market without losing any of the original investment. These types of annuities are called fixed-index annuities and were developed in the 1990s by insurance companies to offer the best benefits of a variable annuity and fixed annuity in one instrument. Here is why they are special . . .

Fixed index annuities grow based on moves in an underlying index, such as the S&P 500. When the market goes up, the value of your annuity goes up. When the market goes down, your annuity will decrease only until the value of your original investment.

The rate of return can never go below zero, and your principal payment is guaranteed. Anything added to the contract value, including premium bonuses or interest credits, is contractually protected from losses. It's a win-win situation, but with a small catch. The upward movements in the stock market are usually capped when it comes to returns for a fixed-index annuity. An insurance company might say that there is a 5% cap on returns or establish a 50% participation rate, which means you will only capture 50% of the total gains in the market. This means if the market goes up 10%, then you will only be credited 5%. It wouldn't make sense for insurance companies to provide unlimited upside with zero downside. So while you sacrifice gains in a really good year, you won't be affected by a 19% drop in the market.

Keep in mind that a fixed-index annuity is not designed to match stock market returns but rather offered as a principal-protected investment with the ability to grow in value. Caps and fees vary from company to company, so it is important to review your options and select the best provider possible. Like CDs, fixed-income annuities require a time commitment, usually three–16 years. However, you can normally withdraw 10% after your first year without penalty.

Another thing to consider with fixed-index annuities are the associated fees. Every year, you will usually be charged an asset or spread fee that detracts from the total value of your returns. For example, if the underlying index gains 12% but the spread fee is 4%, you will only be credited 8% to your account. Investing directly in the market will yield higher returns, but it offers no protection from a fall in the market. A fixed-index annuity, on the other hand, will give you limited upside, but at zero risk to your principal payment. I recommend looking into low-cost fixed-income annuities from T. Rowe Price, Fidelity or AnnuityNet.com. These providers offer low-cost options that allow you to keep your money in your own pocket rather in than the pockets of greedy insurance companies.

Zach's Income Rating: ★★★☆☆

While fixed index annuities are crash proof investments, they should be looked at like insurance products rather than long term buy and hold securities. They have expense fees and generally have low returns even though they are pegged to the market. However, they do offer principal protection on your original investment. Due to expense fees and time requirements, fixed income annuities earn a three star rating.

CHAPTER 23:

HOW TO "PIGGYBACK" CANADIAN SOCIAL SECURITY

In 2015, I discovered an awesome way for Americans to legally "piggyback" Canadian social security to boost their retirement income with quality investments. You won't be collecting checks directly from Canada. However, you will be able to supplement your own Social Security income with one of the best investment opportunities around. It's simple, legal and easy to do. Here is one of the best ways improve your retirement with the help of our northern counterpart.

Similar to U.S. Social Security, the Canada Pension Plan (CPP) is the government program responsible for taking care of Canada's senior citizens. However, instead of taking taxes and storing them in Treasury bonds like the U.S. does, the Canada Pension Plan is run by professional investors that puts Canadian funds in private equity, common stocks, bonds and real estate.

Until recently, the CPP was not like this. Prior to 1996, it operated just as U.S. Social Security does—by taxing the working members of society, storing the funds in bonds and then redistributing money to the elderly. When their analysts determined that the Canadian pension fund would evaporate by 2015, the government took action. They restructured the whole system and began investing the funds into the economy rather than hold them in Treasuries. By doing so, the fund grew rapidly and is now one of the largest pension funds in the world.

The Canada Pension Plan is growing fast, and its analysts spend thousands of hours evaluating the components that go into their portfolio. They purchase whole businesses such as Neiman Marcus and taking large stakes in some of the best companies in the world.

One of the ways they invest is by purchasing common equity—something that anyone can do. Many of the stocks they buy are quality dividend-paying companies that have brought the Canada Pension Plan billions of dollars worth of income. This portfolio is meant to maintain the longevity of the Canadian population, so only the best companies make the cut.

Simply mimic their portfolio (on a much smaller level) and you can collect thousands of dollars from quality investments with high income payments. Mimicking their portfolio is much cheaper than paying a money manager to do the same thing for you. Rather than waste money on commissions and fees, simply buy the companies in your own brokerage account to save thousands while ensuring you are investing in quality companies. By doing so, you will receive a generous amount of income each year to boost your own Social Security payments.

Because the funds are used to support generations of citizens, you can be sure that a great deal of research and analysis was completed for each investment. Piggybacking the Canada Pension Plan's portfolio is a good way to know you are buying quality companies in a diversified manner. In fact, I've helped over 40,000 readers generate income using this strategy.

Here are a few examples of some of the gains we captured in just a few short years:

69% on Extra Space Storage

129% on AbbVie

Or

65% Procter & Gamble

Check out **www.agorafinancial.info/ht479** if you are interested in using this strategy.

Zach's Income Rating: ★★★★★

Piggybacking the Canadian Pension Plan is one of my favorite ways to guarantee you are purchasing quality dividend paying companies. Unlike US Social Security, the Canadian Pension Plan is managed by professional investors that turned a dying pension into one of the strongest retirement programs in the world. If you are looking to manage your own funds, look to the Canadian Pension Plan for guidance.

CHAPTER 24:

HOW TO "HACK" WARREN BUFFETT'S PORTFOLIO AND EARN AN EXTRA $5,233 PER YEAR

After the financial crisis of 2008, most Americans lost their trust in professional money managers. Quite frankly, I don't blame them. The "investment savvy" folks responsible for protecting and growing our wealth twiddled their thumbs while retirement accounts were cut in half.

The managers that claim they will make us fortunes often charge exorbitant fees and produce poor results that a market index could beat. The typical manager is average at best and is more worried about their own commissions rather than the performance of their clients' portfolio.

Today, I'd like to introduce a strategy anyone can use to grow their retirement account without having to use a high-priced manager. It is perfect for those without a financial background, and is far better than risky speculations your neighbor came up with. Best of all, it provides a reliable income source—often bringing in a few hundred to over a thousand dollars a year.

The strategy is simple: Follow the recommendations of Warren Buffett, the most famous value investor in the world. He has amassed a fortune of $84 billion sticking to the same principles over the course of his career. He does not invest in penny stocks looking for risky gains or buy the newest fad exploding in the market. Instead, Warren looks for undervalued companies and lets his wealth grow over time. He is not looking to get rich quick, and patiently collects profits while speculators gamble their funds on the latest boom-and-bust fads. This is a proven strategy that works over time, and you should be using it in your own portfolio.

The idea behind value investing is to buy companies that are priced less than they are worth. Over time, the market will realize they are undervalued, which will cause their prices to increase. This is how investors like Buffett have made billions.

Valuing a company is a tricky process. There is no one correct way to determine the value, so each researcher must use their own analysis to decide what a company is worth. Some analysts put more weight on assets and current book value, while others consider future cash flows to be a more important indicator. Luckily for you, you don't have to complete any analysis to find undervalued companies. Buffett and other famous value investors rarely deviate from their strategies and have done all the work for you—simply look at the companies they invest in. Of course, it is important to do your own due diligence when you want to invest, but looking at Buffett's holdings is a great way to get an idea of a company's worth. On the next page is a list of Berkshire Hathaway's (Buffett's conglomerate) holdings and the income you would receive from holding 100 shares.

It's a lengthy list but a good place to look for moneymaking opportunities that Warren Buffett has put his own money in. If you are interested in learning more about value investing, you should check out *The Intelligent Investor*, by Benjamin Graham. This book is known as the bible of value investing and taught Buffett how to analyze companies. It was originally published in 1949, but remains a best-seller to this day.

If you are wary of giving your money to a professional manager, this strategy is a decent way to search for quality investments. I recommend following the lead of Warren Buffett, the world's greatest value investor, to get an idea of which companies are undervalued. This offers you the chance to find well-run companies without taking expensive advice from professional money managers, all while earning a steady stream of income.

Editor's Note: When we first published the *Big Book of Income*, "hacking" Warren Buffett's portfolio yielded %,233.89 per year. That number has since increased to $6,320.47. The Berhsire Hathaway portfolio as of September 2017 is shown below.

Holdings of Berkshire Hathaway

Symbol	Market Price ($)	Shares	Dividend Yield	Income From 100 Shares	Symbol	Market Price ($)	Shares	Dividend Yield	Income From 100 Shares
AAL	51.12	100	0.78%	39.87	MCO	153.11	100	1%	153.11
AAPL	172.07	100	1.49%	256.38	MDLZ	42.78	100	2.06%	88.13
AXP	99.07	100	1.42%	140.68	MON	117.87	100	1.84%	216.83
AXTA	32.37	100	0%	0.00	MTB	172.01	100	1.75%	301.03
BAC	29.13	100	1.65%	48.06	PG	90.34	100	3.05%	275.54
BK	54.73	100	1.76%	96.32	PSX	99.93	100	2.81%	280.80
CHTR	328.07	100	0%	0.00	QSR	60.48	100	1.30%	78.62
COST	188.25	100	1.06%	199.55	SIRI	5.68	100	0.78%	4.43
DAL	54.40	100	2.28%	124.03	SNY	43.90	100	3.79%	166.38
DVA	69.89	100	0%	0.00	STOR	25.87	100	4.81%	124.43
GHC	571.25	100	0.90%	514.13	SYF	34.62	100	1.60%	60.19
GM	41.47	100	3.61%	149.71	TMK	89.27	100	0.67%	59.81
GS	253.38	100	1.20%	304.06	UAL	64.14	100	0%	0.00
IBM	156.78	100	3.89%	609.87	UPS	117.94	100	2.78%	327.87
JNJ	142.98	100	2.40%	343.15	USB	55.33	100	2.19%	121.17
KHC	78.80	100	3.19%	251.37	USG	36.87	100	0%	0.00
KO	45.39	100	3.27%	148.43	V	112.88	100	0.70%	79.02
LBTYA	32.24	100	0%	0.00	VRSK	93.97	100	0%	0.00
LBTYK	31.40	100	0%	0.00	VRSN	114.48	100	0%	0.00
LILA	21.60	100	0%	0.00	VZ	52.93	100	4.62%	24.54
LILAK	21.39	100	0%	0.00	WFC	59.44	100	2.63%	156.33
LSXMA	43.01	100	0%	0.00	WMT	96.75	100	2.11%	204.14
LUV	63.75	100	0.79%	50.36	**Total**	**447,854.00**	**100**	**1.54%**	**6,320.47**
MA	152.44	100	0.67%	102.13					

As of September 2017, Source: cnbc.com

Zach's Income Rating: ★★★☆☆

One of the best ways to manage your own portfolio is to take advice from one of the greatest value investors to ever live—Warren Buffett. This strategy is great if you want to cut the middle man and save on wealth management fees. Best of all, most of the companies in his portfolio pay dividends. Using Warren's advice is good as a starting point, but you should do you own due diligence when researching a company. Never blindly follow someone else's lead.

CHAPTER 25:

GET PAID EVERY TIME "YOUR" SONG GETS PLAYED ON THE RADIO

As you are listening to the radio driving down the highway, a familiar song graces your ears:

Imagine all the people . . .

It's been over 40 years since John Lennon released "Imagine," in 1971, but did you know his estate still gets paid every time the song is played? In fact, every time you hear a song on the radio, the artist collects a royalty for the use of their music.

Through a little-known website, you can actually start collecting these royalties yourself. Anything from John Lennon's "Imagine" to the *Caddyshack* theme song—each recording charges a fee to use its song. Today, you can become an owner of these famous labels and claim a royalty every time the song is played.

By becoming a member of royalty exchange (royaltyexchange.com), you can actually purchase the rights to famous songs by bidding in an online auction.

Essentially, the rights are up for auction because the artist is looking for a lump sum of cash needed for the short term. If Bruce Springsteen wanted some cash, he could put up the rights for "Born in the U.S.A." up for auction. Then anytime that song was played on the radio or featured some-where, the buyer of the rights would receive the royalties for that song.

Recent auctions include Barry White's "You're the First, the Last, My Everything" and the royalties of jazz legend Walter Beasley.

The royalties you purchase last for the life of the contract, sometimes over 75 years! These royalties are stable investments that provide con-sistent year-round income. Depending on the nature of the contract, the royalty is paid either quarterly or biyearly.

Each auction will have different terms. For example, one royalty may be for one year, while another may be 50% of the royalties for the life of the artist.

Signing up is easy.

Simply enter your email address, password and phone number and you can create an account. Then you can browse auctions and view their specifications.

Royalty Exchange will post all pertinent information, including finan-cial performance of the royalty in the past.

I should let you know that these royalty streams can cost several thou-sand dollars upfront. However, the returns can be extraordinary.

Check out royaltyexchange.com for more information.

Zach's Income Rating: ★★★☆☆

While purchasing the rights to songs on Royalty Exchange can lead to a lucrative income stream, the startup costs are usually significant. To participate in this opportunity, you may need at least ten thousand dollars depending on the opportunity. Sometimes, the royalties up for auction are limited. For these reasons, this opportunity receives three stars.

CHAPTER 26:

THE SECRET REAL ESTATE INVESTMENT WITH GUARANTEED RETURNS

One of the best kept secrets of the investing world comes in the form of little-known real estate investments called tax liens or tax deeds. These obscure investments are auctioned off by the government and essentially guarantee a high-yield return if investors do their research on the terms of the lien. In most cases, these investments bring in 15–25% returns with very little risk involved. Liens and deeds differ slightly in mechanics, but they are acquired and offer returns in a very similar fashion.

The way tax liens work is simple. Every homeowner must pay property taxes, but sometimes they fall behind on payments. The government does not like this because they have built a budget including everyone's property taxes. At first, they charge the homeowner interest, but if payment is not made before a certain date, a lien is issued and auctioned off to the general public. The government wants its money, and this gives investors the chance to purchase the lien (i.e., pay the delinquent taxes for the homeowner) in exchange for a handsome interest rate. When the homeowner finally pays the taxes, the investor gets their money back plus interest.

If the property owner does not pay off their tax bill by the due date, one of two things will happen: The home will either become the investor's property or be sold at public auction with a starting bid to cover all taxes and fees, which would then be used to pay off the lien.

You see, it's a win-win scenario any way you look at it. If the homeowner pays the fee, then you, the investor, just made a solid return on your investment. If the homeowner doesn't don't pay, their property becomes yours or the auction winner pays the lien.

Best of all, a tax lien is considered a first-position lien, and the lien holder will receive compensation from the collateral even before mortgages. That means you are in front of the banks when it comes time to collect payments.

Typically, the homeowner will come up with payment before the house is seized, so property transfer is rare. In any case, it is a great chance for you to make a good return on your money. Tax liens are offered in the following states:

Alabama
Arizona
Colorado
Florida
Maryland
Montana
Nebraska
New Jersey
South Dakota
Wyoming

Tax deeds are similar to tax liens, but instead of purchasing the right to owed taxes, you are bidding directly on a property. In most cases, the starting bid on a tax deed is simply the value of the owed taxes. With tax deeds, the focus is more on becoming the owner of the foreclosed house, which you can then sell for a profit. Through tax deed investing, you can end up owning a home for pennies on the dollar. Again, the auction process is very similar to the tax liens process.

Tax deed are offered in the following states:

Alaska

Arkansas

California

Florida

Idaho

Kansas

Michigan

Nevada

New Mexico

New York

North Dakota

Ohio

Oklahoma

Utah

Virginia

Washington

Both of these little-known investments made possible through government auctions essentially guarantee a return for investors at a high yield. Properly using this technique can bring investors fortunes, and today, I will show you how to complete the transaction yourself.

It is relatively uncommon way of investing because of how difficult it used to be to accomplish. In fact, the only way to invest in tax liens just a few years ago was to show up at a courthouse and bid on liens at auction. Today, investing in tax liens and tax deeds is easier than ever. The internet has made it possible to successfully invest without having to call courthouses or attend auctions featuring meager properties.

The first thing you want to establish is if your state and local government have tax lien or tax deed policies. Remember, with tax lien investing, you look to get high returns on interest rates—in other words, to receive payment on the taxes rather than own a property in the rare case of property transfer. Tax deed investors are looking to score a property for pennies on the dollar, and then flip the house for major returns.

Once you have familiarized yourself with local laws, here is how you can break into the tax lien and tax deed investing scene.

Most of the time, counties that offer tax liens will have a list of available liens on their government website. If your county does not have an online resource, contact the county tax lien representative and ask if you can have the list of liens mailed to your home.

You can then look up the properties you are interested in on the property appraiser's website. This will give you valuable information, such as past property taxes and how much the house was sold for on previous dates. Websites such as Google Maps and Zillow will also show you more pictures of the property and include other valuable facts.

Once you have narrowed down your properties of interest, you can attend the auction by bidding online through your county website or through the local courthouse. Since every region is different, I recommend researching the procedures in your area or contacting the local government for more information. This way, you can confirm whether bidding takes place online or if you must attend an auction in person.

While every county will have different policies, investing in tax deeds is a great way to get a low-risk, high-return investment in your own community. These investments frequently average a 15–25% return on your investment. Either one makes a great choice for investing, and I recommend you research more to find what's right for you.

Warning: If you don't do your own due diligence, it can be easy to get into trouble with tax liens. If you do not properly research a property, you won't know its true value. In some cases, the property could be in an inaccessible area, or be in an undesirable area such as on a patch of grass by the highway or in swamplands, rendering it worthless.

Zach's Income Rating: ★★★★☆

Tax liens and tax deeds are little known investments that offer high returns with often little risk. The issue with these investments is that you must complete hours of research to know the true value of the property you are looking at. If you purchase a lien, but are second to other liens, you may lose money on your investment.

CHAPTER 27:

MEET THE BANK THAT GIVES A 3% INTEREST RATE ON SAVINGS

If you aren't yet earning the highest interest in America, that's about to quickly change. American savers are in luck, because these high-interest accounts are available in every state in the country—in most counties, with 8,308 options nationwide. Starting today, I'll guarantee an interest rate 16 times the national average, which currently hovers around 0.06%. Even better, you could claim interest rates on regular checking and savings accounts up to 7.5%!

Now let me break this down . . . In 2008, the Federal Reserve took interest rates down to zero. This was to force Americans out of their savings accounts and into riskier investments such as stocks. That way, the new inflow of money would prop up the stock market. And that trick worked for the Federal Reserve . . .

That meant Americans weren't earning interest on their savings accounts. The only way they could make their money work was through less desirable and riskier investments. For older Americans, this was a nightmare. There comes a time when keeping your money in savings accounts is the right thing to do. There is VERY little risk when you have your money in a bank account. And you SHOULD be able to receive a small, yet sizable portion of interest. The Federal Reserve took away the ability to earn interest . . . Until today.

Right now, there is a way to get interest rates not seen since before the financial crisis of 2008, when bank accounts paid out modest sums. Today, I am guaranteeing you can find 1–7.5% interest for regular checking and savings accounts, that are FDIC or NCUA insured up to $250,000. I'm talking about the holy grail of interest. Liquid cash in a bank account that isn't tied down by the terms of some CD, that is earning interest rates not seen since before the financial crisis.

Now, this may sound unconventional, but there have been a plethora of high-interest accounts popping up in the U.S. thanks to new-age financial consulting and service firms. However, these financial consulting firms cannot advertise the locations of where they offer these high-interest accounts, because the local banks and credit unions would be charged higher insurance rates, therefore making higher interest impossible to offer. Despite the complications, don't fret.

I'll explain everything. One of the largest brands of high-interest consulting brands is Kasasa, based out of Austin, Texas. Kasasa is a wholesale financial services company that engineers products to drive profit and growth for community financial institutions. Essentially, they provide banks and credit unions with marketing and the tools needed to attract and maintain customers, while the local banks themselves can offer Kasasa brand accounts.

If you added up all of the deposits in Kasasa-branded accounts, they would be the fifth-largest bank in all of the U.S. Instead, they are at local community banks and credit unions, teaming up to "win the war" against the mega banks! So how does Kasasa help banks pay out abnormal interest rates? Well, it's quite simple.

The local bank pays Kasasa a fee for their financial services. This includes the use of their brand and marketing tools. These tools also include high-interest bank accounts. Customers come to the bank for high interest . . . but they also use the bank for other needs, such as mortgages and auto loans. This means that the local bank or credit union profits from the increase in foot traffic. More loans equal more business.

Kasasa isn't the only brand of high-interest account. And unless you belong to a specific bank or credit union, you would likely have no idea that these accounts are available. The big banks have been screwing us for years. Americans deserve higher interest. It's not right that we earn no money holding our money in a bank. And it's even worse that we have to look at risky investments to get a return on our money.

Here is what I recommend . . . Google Kasasa and the name of your hometown, or go to depositaccounts.com to see if any high-interest accounts are in your area.

When you find an appropriate bank, check with their policies regarding these accounts. Most of the accounts require that you complete a certain number of debit card transactions each month (eight–12), and there may be a limit on the dollar amount for the supercharged interest. For example, a policy through one credit union might be 4% on the first $10,000 and then a lower rate on anything else. This will depend on the location in which you sign up, but a simple way around this problem is to open multiple accounts at different branches—check with your local bank to see if that's an option!

Another issue you might encounter with these special accounts is the number of debit purchases you must complete per month in order to maintain the interest. However, this can be easily remedied. Since the dollar amount of the purchases will not matter in many cases, you can buy very cheap items on Amazon.com. Amazon has a plethora of items ranging from less than a buck all the way down to a single penny.

Think of little knickknacks, cards, toys, rubber bands or other household items you might need. Amazon will most likely have a VERY cheap version that will allow you complete the required number of purchases, which will allow you to easily maintain the high interest on your account.

The terms for each account are different, so be sure to look over the terms of the bank account to know exactly what you need to do. While it might be a small inconvenience, the high interest you receive on these accounts makes it well worth your effort.

And remember, your money is FDIC or NCUA insured up to $250,000. So don't delay, and start your brand-new high-interest account today.

Zach's Income Rating: ★★★★★

Kasasa bank is an FDIC insured bank that offers interest rates at least 12 times greater than average. Some accounts require you to have direct deposit and use your debit card a few times a month. But for those looking to earn interest in a safe place, Kasasa is a great choice.

CHAPTER 28:

ONE SIMPLE TRICK TO "BOOST" YOUR SOCIAL SECURITY BENEFITS BY $570 PER MONTH

According to the Center for Retirement Research at Boston College, over 97% of Americans do not receive the maximum amount of Social Security benefits allowed by law. In many cases, Americans are forgoing over $150,000 in lifetime benefits—an astronomical figure for any social class. Today, I'd like to show you the one simple way to ensure you receive all of the money you are entitled to, and it all starts with one word:

Void.

If you are under the age of 70 and plan on filing for Social Security, "voiding" your application is a crucial step in getting every benefit you are entitled to.

The problem is that most Americans think of Social Security as something you simply sign up for when you want to retire after a certain age. The truth is "signing up" for Social Security can be an extremely complex process, and most Americans are missing out on benefits they didn't know are available to them.

The first issue begins with the length of the Social Security handbook. There are 2,738 grueling sections which make it nearly impossible to read and digest. Filled with rules, strategies, caveats and restrictions, it's no wonder even informed Americans still make the wrong filing decisions.

There are hundreds of books out there on how to file and maximize your benefits, but the truth is that maximizing your benefits is based on one simple factor. In this chapter, I'll discuss how you can use this factor to maximize your retirement checks. There are many different ways to get the most out of Social Security, but this single technique has the ability to raise your lifetime benefits by hundreds of thousands of dollars. In fact, it is one of the easiest ways to increase your payments as well.

WHY AGE MATTERS

The age at which you decide to file for Social Security is one of the most crucial decisions you can make for your retirement income. In order to claim your full, regular Social Security benefits, you must be 66 years old. This is called "full retirement age." If you aren't aware, your benefits can either increase or decrease based on your age.

You can claim your benefits as early as 62 years old or at any age after. However, for each year you claim early (before 66 years of age), there is a percentage deducted from your monthly payment, reducing your total benefits. For example, if your full retirement benefits would be $1,000 a month at 66 years of age and you claimed early at 62, you would receive $750 a month instead of the full payment. This penalty may not seem like much, but it makes a big difference for your total lifetime benefits.

On the other hand, for every year you wait after full retirement age, your benefits grow by 8% a year, up until the age of 70. Now, 8% might not seem like much growth, but if you look at the chart on the next page, you will see how significantly your benefits can rise if you wait. Each line represents how much money you would receive based on the age at which you file.

You can see from the graph that if you expect to live 82 years, filing at 70 can significantly raise your lifetime benefits. Over the course of your life, it can add up to hundreds of thousands of dollars in extra income.

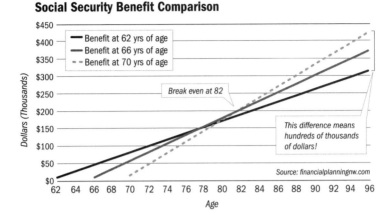

Social Security Benefit Comparison

From our example before, it's the difference between $750 a month at 62 or $1,320 at 70. That's an extra $570 a month!

The simple lesson is that the later you file, the greater your benefits. If you don't mind holding off on taking your Social Security checks, then I recommend waiting in order to maximize the amount you can receive from the government. However, everyone's situation is different, and filling at an earlier time might be best depending on the circumstances.

Filing early is a good strategy if you are in desperate need of income or in a situation that reduces your life expectancy. Maybe you just are unsure of the future and feel better taking the money while it is offered. However, if you can, delaying your payments until you are 70 is by far the most efficient way to maximize your lifetime benefits.

After you are 70, your benefits cannot grow any further. Therefore, 70 should be the latest age at which you file. Any later date is a waste, because your payments can no longer grow.

If you file when you are 70, by the time you reach 82 years of age, you will have already made up the income you would have received by delaying payments. After that, the extra income keeps adding up. If you are healthy and expect to live past 82, it makes no sense to claim benefits early when the value added from waiting is so high. In fact, by delaying payments, you can increase your benefits by 76%. Take note of this strategy and discuss the benefits with your financial adviser. This is one of the easiest ways to increase your lifetime benefits by over $100,000.

Zach's Income Rating: ★★★★☆

Delaying your Social Security benefits is one of the best ways boost your retirement income by tens of thousands, if not hundreds of thousands of dollars. If you are over 70 years old, or need Social Security as a base income, you cannot take advantage of this filing strategy.

CHAPTER 29:

BEAT THE IRS AT ITS OWN GAME— A QUICK GUIDE TO MANDATORY DISTRIBUTIONS, REDUCING TAXES AND MORE

No one does a better job at taking Americans' hard-earned cash than the U.S. government. Every paycheck, a large chunk of money is taken out to pay for mismanaged projects and dead-end proposals. They can't fix the potholes, Social Security has been mismanaged and health insurance costs a fortune. What exactly do they do with all of that money?

No one but the government can answer that question. Luckily, there are little-known ways to reduce the amount you owe to the government that few take advantage of. All it takes is a few simple steps—and you can legally reduce the amount you pay the IRS.

In order for these strategies to work, you must know the basic differences between the retirement accounts that offer tax advantages. You must also be aware of required minimum distributions, which are mandatory withdrawals from retirement accounts after the age of 70.5 years of age.

I'll explain everything in the sections below, but first, let's start off with the differences in retirement accounts and why knowing their provisions can save you thousands in taxes.

UNDERSTANDING RETIREMENT ACCOUNTS AND REQUIRED MINIMUM DISTRIBUTIONS

Of the many retirement accounts an individual can use, the most popular are the traditional 401(k), Roth IRA, traditional IRA and Roth 401(k). The names are similar and may be hard to differentiate, but after comparing them side by side, it is easy to see what attributes correspond with each particular account. It is important to know how they vary because they have different rules regarding taxes and distributions.

To make things simple, think of things this way: If the account has "Roth" in front of it, you deposit your post-tax earnings and they grow tax free. That means when you withdraw after a certain age, you won't pay a cent in capital gains tax or income tax. (Since Roth funds are already taxed, this isn't the money the government is after.)

For the traditional IRA and 401(k), your initial deposit is from pretax dollars or is tax deductible, and then you pay income tax when you withdraw after a certain age.

The chart below compares the accounts according to their tax requirements when you deposit and withdraw:

Account Type	Deposit	Withdraw	RMD
IRA	Tax Deductible	Pay Income Tax	Yes
Roth IRA	Post Tax Income	Tax Free	No
401(k)	Pre Tax Income	Pay Income Tax	Yes
Roth 401(k)	Post Tax Income	Tax Free	No

Now, you might be wondering, what is an "RMD"? This stands for required minimum distribution, which means seniors are forced to take money out of their retirement accounts and pay tax on the withdrawal.

Mandatory withdrawals are another part of our government's' "war on savers." They are to ensure individuals aren't using retirement accounts as a vehicle to pass inheritance and to forcefully generate tax revenue for the U.S. government.

As an example, the general "uniform" minimum distribution can be found using the table on the next page. To determine your required minimum distribution, divide your total retirement account value by the distribution period found next to your age.

Uncle Sam Is Coming For Your Savings!
Required Minimum Distributions For IRAs

Age of retiree	Distribution period (in yrs)	Age of retiree	Distribution period (in yrs)
70	27.4	93	9.6
71	20.5	94	9.1
72	25.6	95	8.6
73	24.7	96	8.1
74	23.8	97	7.6
75	22.9	98	7.1
76	22.9	99	6.7
77	21.2	100	6.3
78	20.3	101	5.9
79	19.5	102	5.5
80	18.7	103	5.2
81	17.9	104	4.9
82	17.1	105	4.5
83	16.3	106	4.2
84	15.5	107	3.9
85	14.8	108	3.7
86	14.1	109	3.4
87	13.4	110	3.1
88	12.7	111	2.9
89	12.0	112	2.6
90	11.4	113	2.4
91	10.8	114	2.1
92	10.2	115 +	1.0

Source: irs.gov

For example, if you are 72 years old and have a $400,000 retirement account, divide $400,000 by 25.6 to get $15,625 as a minimum distribution. That means you MUST take out $15,625 for the current year and pay taxes like it was regular income. If you do not complete the withdrawal, you will face a 50% fine on the amount that was supposed to be taken out. If you are nearing age 70 and weren't aware of these distributions, this is not something you want to ignore.

HOW TO MAXIMIZE YOUR WEALTH BY REDUCING TAXES

Now that you are up to speed on retirement accounts and RMDs, you can use this knowledge to lower your tax bill.

To successfully lower your tax bill, you need to strategically withdraw from your accounts to reduce the amount that can be forced out due to RMDs once you turn 70.5. If you have a lower balance in accounts that can be taxed, your minimum distributions will be lower, which means you will pay less in taxes.

Here is how this strategy works:

Of the four accounts mentioned above, the only type of account that doesn't require a minimum distribution is the Roth IRA. Therefore, the goal is to get as much of your retirement savings into a Roth IRA from the ages of 59.5 to 70.5.

Why 59.5? That's when you can access your retirement accounts without penalty and you can begin to transfer funds as freely as you'd like.

Deciding how much to roll over is the hard part. Typically, you can roll over a portion or the entire balance of a 401(k) or traditional IRA into a Roth IRA, but you must pay taxes when that rollover occurs. For most people, rolling over their entire account that would take them into a higher tax bracket, which is exactly what we want to avoid.

What you need to do is maximize your current tax bracket, meaning your yearly income reaches the maximum allowed limit within your current bracket. This is actually much easier than it sounds. Take a look at the 2016 Estimated Income Tax Brackets below:

2018 Estimated Income Tax Brackets

Rate	Single Fillers	Married Joint Fillers	Head of Household Fillers
10%	Not over $9,525	Not over $19,050	Not over $13,600
15%	$9,525 to $38,700	$19,050 to $77,400	$13,600 to $51,850
25%	$38,700 to $93,700	$77,400 to $156,150	$51,95 to $133,850
28%	$93,700 to $195,450	$156,150 to $237,950	$133,850 to $216,700
33%	$195,450 to $424,950	$237,950 to $424,950	$216,700 to $424,950
35%	$424,950 to $426,700	$424,950 to $480,050	$424,950 to $453,350
39.6%	Over $426,700	Over $480,050	Over $453,350

Source: taxfoundation.org

Say you are 59.5 years old, single and bring in $150,000 a year. You are currently in the 28% tax bracket, which extends all the way up to $195,450. That means any extra income you bring in up to $195,450 will be taxed at 28%, and anything greater will be taxed at 33%. In this situation, I would transfer $45,450 from your traditional retirement account and put it into a Roth IRA.

This way, you are maximizing your tax bracket and your money will grow tax free for as long as you hold it in the Roth IRA. Because you already paid taxes, your money will grow tax free, and you will not be forced to withdraw in the future.

This is especially lucrative if you think your income is going to rise, because you would pay less taxes now than you would in the future. If you do this each year, your required minimum distributions will be much less than they would be. By the time you retire, the tax savings could be close to half of a year's salary.

Rolling over is easy. You simply contact the manager of your 401(k) or IRA and tell them you want to roll funds over to the account of your choice. Usually, they will complete the transaction for you, but sometimes they will send you a check for the amount you want to roll over and you will have 60 days to deposit the funds into your new account.

If this seems complicated, speak with a financial adviser for advice on how to reduce taxes through a Roth conversion. Remember, this strategy may not be for everyone, so I cannot guarantee this is right for you.

If you were curious about other ways to save on taxes, I've listed further information below.

GENERAL TIPS FOR MINIMIZING TAXES AND MAXIMIZING WEALTH

1. **If You Are Working and in a Higher Tax Bracket, Contribute to a Traditional IRA—** A traditional IRA allows you to put money into a retirement account and deduct your contributions from your current income. This is great if you have a high tax bracket right now because it minimizes the taxes you pay today and leaves more of your income available for you to invest and grow your money. The nice thing about a traditional IRA is that you can use just about any income strategy to generate extra money within your IRA. This year, individuals can contribute $5,500 to an IRA, and if you're age 50 or over, you can contribute as much as $6,500 per year.

2. **If You Are Working and in a Lower Tax Bracket, Contribute to a Roth IRA—**The good thing about a Roth IRA is that no matter how much your account grows, you'll never have to pay a dime of taxes on the money again. The downside is that your Roth IRA

contributions are not tax deductible right now. But if you're in a low tax bracket, it makes more sense to pay some small taxes today and have your Roth IRA money grow without ever having to pay tax again. Just like a traditional IRA, you can use almost any income strategy in this type of account as well.

3. **Consider Education Savings Accounts**—If you're looking forward to paying education costs for a student in your life, a 529 savings plan can help you save on taxes. While contributions to a 529 plan are not tax deductible, the growth in your 529 plan is not taxable. Also, there are specific tax savings from individual states, so check to determine what rules and breaks your state offers.

These strategies do a great job of helping you get your money into a place where the government can't touch it—or at least where the government has minimal ability to tax what is rightfully yours. But did you know that how you invest in your individual accounts can also make a big difference in your tax bill? Here are a few key strategies to keep in mind:

Use Short-Term or Instant Income Strategies in Tax-Sheltered Account—This strategy goes against the way many traditional money managers think. You've probably heard that you should use your IRA for long-term investment opportunities like buying and holding dividend stocks. But you can save thousands in tax bills if you use your IRA for our "instant income" strategies like selling covered calls or selling put contracts.

When you make money using these strategies, the government typically taxes your profits at the same rate that normal income is taxed. However, if you use these strategies in your IRA or Roth IRA, you'll be deferring (or eliminating) high taxes on these profits.

Use Taxable Accounts for Dividend Stocks—Did you know that your dividends are typically taxed at a lower rate? Plus, investors typically hold dividend stocks for more than a year, which means when you sell for a profit, you are taxed at a lower rate for those profits as well. If you have money in a taxable account, this is the best option for purchasing dividend stocks. You'll wind up paying less taxes each year, which leaves you to keep more of your hard-earned money.

Max out Your 401(k) Match—This may sound pretty straightforward, but a surprising number of Americans don't take advantage of this lucrative opportunity. Many employers have a match program that literally gives you **free** money when you contribute your own money to your company's retirement program, which is essentially an instant 50% or 100% return on your money. It goes without saying that you should contribute as much as possible to these programs until you're collecting every "free" dollar possible. The money that goes into your 401(k) is pretax income, so you are earning tax free dollars when your employer matches (just remember you will be taxed when you withdraw).

When it comes time to pay the tax bill, the above tips can be extremely useful in reducing what you owe to the government. I recommend discussing the tips on how to properly withdraw or transfer funds in order to stay within the same tax bracket with your financial adviser. Everyone's situation is different, but hopefully, some of these tips will allow you to keep some of your hard-earned cash that would have otherwise gone to Uncle Sam. If you're still saving money for retirement, these strategies may be extremely lucrative. Be advised everyone's tax situation is different, so make sure to consult a tax professional before making any decisions.

Zach's Income Rating: ★★★☆☆

While these strategies can maximize the money you keep from the government, they require a bit of planning on the part of the individual and can take years to take advantage of. Additionally, they are not a source of consistent income, therefore this opportunity is rated as three stars.

Hey, Zach Scheidt stopping in!

I hope you've been enjoying my *Big Book of Income* so far, and have used some of these ideas to boost your daily cash flow.

But I have a favor to ask you...

If you have a second, would you stop by **sites.agorafinancial.com/LIR/BigBookSurvey** and let me know what you think of the book?

I want real feedback telling me what chapters you've used, and how much income you've been able to generate.

Thanks in advance!

Here's to growing your income,

Zach Scheidt

IV. HOBBIES THAT PAY

This section shows how to turn your hobbies into paychecks, turn unwanted junk into cash and actually win in the casino. For these strategies, a greater time commitment is required, but the rewards are substantial.

CHAPTER 30:

URBAN TREASURE HUNTING— MAKE MONEY FROM "BURIED" LOOT IN YOUR OWN NEIGHBORHOOD

Urban treasure hunting is an exciting hobby that can provide extra cash or real, hold-in-your-hand treasures without having to go far from your own home. Whether you live in a country town or populated city, urban treasure hunting can be done almost anywhere.

The secret is that from garage sales to thrift shops, grocery stores and even banks, there are ways to find precious metals for little to no cost—you just have to know where to look. These secrets might land you a few hundred or even thousands of dollars in valuable finds.

Let's start with one of the most important steps in looking for precious metals: how to tell if they are real—without going to the experts.

#1 BECOME A HUMAN METAL DETECTOR (LEARN HOW TO TELL WHAT'S PRECIOUS AND WHAT'S NOT)

One of the most dumbfounding things about precious metals is that they can be right under your nose and you don't even realize it. If you had a hunk of silver, you wouldn't throw it away, would you? Grandpa's old platter, a couple of spoons or even an old button that you ended up selling at the garage sale for a few dollars could have been worth a fortune had you just done a simple test.

Many times, people "give away" their precious metals because they don't know how much they are worth—and that is dollars down the drain. With the tips you learn today, you will be able to determine the makeup of an object whether it is in your own house, in a jewelry store or at your local garage sale.

HOUSEHOLD ITEMS THAT GRADE LIKE A PRO

You are about to have a garage sale, and grandpa's platter is sitting over on the table. You don't know what a fair price is, so you decide it's worth $50 for the sentimental value. The platter is sold, and you are happy to get your $50. The buyer is also happy, because he just got platter made of 150 ounces of fine silver worth over $2,000.

Don't let this happen. Many items in your house are probably made of silver that you aren't aware of. Silver is a common material in antiques and old coins, so the more knowledge you have, the better off you are at finding hidden treasures.

Antiques may be hard to judge, but coins are some of the easiest items to examine on sight. In general, dimes, quarters, half dollars and dollars minted before 1965 are made of silver. So if you see any of these in an old stash of coins, take them out, because they are worth way more than their face value.

For other objects, have no fear. A few simple tests conducted in your own house can give you a ballpark estimate of their value. The household items below could make you hundreds of dollars by helping determine what your items are made of.

Magnifying Glass—This is perhaps one of the most important tools on this list, as you will always want to examine the object before going on to other tests. Many times, objects made of precious metals will be stamped or contain identifying marks giving you clues as to its value. If the object in question is believed to be silver, use your magnifying glass to find any mark that says "999" or "Fine Silver." This is the most pure type of silver and therefore the most valuable. The second most valuable type of silver is sterling silver, which should be stamped with a "925," meaning that it is 92.5% silver and 7.5% copper.

When looking at gold, markings are also an indication of what the metal is made of. Normally, you will see the following:

10K, 10ct or 416, which is 41.6% gold
12K, 10ct or 500, which is 50% gold
14K, 14ct or 585, which is 58.5% gold
15K, 15ct or 625, which is 62.5% gold
18K, 18ct or 750, which is 75% gold
22K, 22ct or 916, which is 91.6% gold
24K, 24ct or 1000, which is 100% gold.

You might also see GEP, RGP, HGE or HGP, which means the gold is electroplated. Electroplated gold is not solid gold throughout—there are just a few particles of gold on the outside of the jewelry. If the gold is made in a country that requires stamping, then these markings are generally accurate. But beware: The marking is only as honest as the jeweler, so additional tests would be helpful to guarantee authenticity.

Even if there are no markings, the magnifying glass can be helpful in looking for discoloration, which is another way to determine the contents of the object. Many times, silver will tarnish or develop a patina, which is a rich, dark or multicolored film on the surface of the object. Check out the patina on the coin below:

A Patina Is a Sign It's Silver. Source: Wikicommons

Patinas are valuable, and this is another sign that the object could be silver. On the other hand, gold should be one color. There may be tarnish if the gold is alloyed with other metals, but if the edges are worn and changing colors, it could be an indication that the metal is gold plated or is made of a variety of metals.

Magnet—A magnet is a useful tool because precious metals such as gold and silver are nonferrous, or nonmagnetic, materials. If an object in question is attracted to the magnet, then it is most likely not a precious metal. Fine silver, sterling silver and high-karat gold will not be magnetic. If an object is magnetic, then it is probably plated or entirely fake. The only caveat is that 10-karat and 14-karat gold items may contain nickel, which is a magnetic material. From my experience, these types of golds will not be extremely magnetic, so use your best judgement when testing your metals.

Now, just because a silvery object does not stick to the magnet does not mean its silver. Other types of nonferrous materials could have been used to make the object in question, but it certainly narrows down the field.

Testing Kits—If the silver or gold in question is your own, then it might be beneficial to buy cheap testing solutions, which you can get on-line for as little as $4. Testing kits should come with a stone or dark plate on which you can rub part of the object and apply the testing solution. This way, you don't have to apply the testing solution to the object itself. Because the solutions are acidic (typically nitric acid), they will deface the metal if you apply them directly. However, if you can find an inconspicuous location on the object, you may use the solution sparingly. Here is how the tests work:

For silver, rub the object in question on the stone and then apply the testing solution. After you apply it, you should see a color change within a few moments. According to the color, you will have an idea of what your object is. Check out the chart below to see what the color changes represent if you are using a standard nitric acid test.

Color scale of your specific silver test

Bright red	Fine silver
Darker red	925 silver
Brown	800 silver
Green	500 silver
Yellow	Lead or tin
Dark Brown	Brass
Blue	Nickel

Source: gemology.com

For gold, the kit is a bit more sophisticated. Instead of one testing solution, you get four bottles, and each tests a different karat of gold. The bottles will be typically be labeled according to the type of gold they identify—22 karat, 18 karat, 14 karat and 10 karat. The way these solutions work is simple. If the object in question reacts with the testing solution, than its karat is less that the karat listed on the label.

Remember, you should use these tests only with your own valuables. A person at a garage sale or salesman at a jewelry store would not appreciate you scratching their items or putting acid on them.

When it comes to testing precious metals, stick with the official kits in order to get the most accurate results. If you have seen other ways of testing made popular through the internet, such as with makeup or ice, be warned that these kinds of tests can lead to inaccurate results.

Now that you know the secrets, it is time to start testing objects in your own home. Those random forks and knives in the cabinet or the old plate that was given to you could easily be worth a decent amount of money. Before your next yard sale, go into your attic and use these strategies on things you might consider junk. You don't want your trash to become another man's treasure.

You can also use these techniques at thrift stores and garage sales to confirm or deny your suspicions of various objects. That way, you will have greater knowledge when purchasing something and know if you are getting the right deal.

#2 FREE GOLD AT THE GROCERY STORE

When my colleague told me the details of his newest project, I couldn't help but listen in disbelief. He told me he can get free gold at any grocery store, and I immediately doubted the story—until I saw the results from his hunting. Silver dimes and quarters, Morgan silver dollars, even a pair of gold earrings—all from local grocery stores around his home. Right now is a great time to try this strategy out because not many people know this secret. Here is how it works:

Just about every grocery store in the country has a way for their patrons to get paper bills for their coins. You might know them as a Coinstar machines. These machines offer a slot in which to dump loose change in exchange for cash. It certainly beats rolling up coins and taking them to the bank.

Here is where the secret lies . . . When people dump their change, typically from an old tub or large coffee can, they unknowingly put silver coins into the machine. If you have ever been to your grandma's house and gone through the coin jar, you will know what I am talking about. Since the machine doesn't recognize silver, oddly weighted coins or foreign currency, it will process everything except those objects. The rejected coins are then sent to the return slot, where people will scoop them up and run them through the machine again. A lot of times, people end up leaving the silver there because they think they are leaving a couple dimes that can't be processed. And while that secret can lead you to find some interesting coins, there is a way to get even greater returns from the Coinstar machine.

When you dump coins into the machine, there is a grate below the coin slot to prevent things like lint and small pieces of dirt from going into the machine. Underneath the grate is a collection bin for the foreign debris and large items that make their way into the Coinstar machine.

Many times, large silver dollars won't be recognized by Coinstar and *will not* be returned to the customer. Instead, they will end up in the debris pile underneath the grate. Besides silver dollars, this debris pile will collect earrings, wedding rings and other valuables that make their way into the machine. You would think people would be more responsible, but it is actually quite common for jewelry to end up in the Coinstar. All it takes is a night out on the town and accidentally placing your earrings in the coin jar.

You can imagine how the wildest things can end up going through those slots. Take a look with your cellphone flashlight next time you go in. If you see something, here is how you can get it out:

The person at the customer service desk of the grocery store actually has a key to the Coinstar machine. Periodically, they are supposed to empty the tray that gets filled with junk. If you bring a reusable shopping bag and politely ask if they will fill it with the contents from the Coinstar machine while you go shopping, most of the time, they will oblige. When you get home, empty the contents, put on some gloves and search for interesting items. Then, you can go through the testing procedures and see what you have come up with. Just remember it takes time for the contents to fall in, so don't be impatient and frequently visit the same places over and over. Wait a while and you will reap the rewards without making too many requests for the employees.

#3 FREE SILVER FROM BANKS AND CASINOS

By far the easiest way to get free silver is by going to your local bank or casino and asking one simple question. It is so effective that these banks and casinos will give you free silver without even realizing it. The key here is a trick called coin roll hunting, and it has netted many with troves of silver finds. Here is how the system works . . .

Remember, dimes, quarters, half dollars and dollars that were minted before 1965 are made of silver. Most cashiers and bank tellers know this, so when they see a silver coin, they keep it, taking it out of circulation. However, there is a caveat. How often do you get a half dollar as change or even use half dollars? The answer for most people is almost never.

Another treasure hunting tip most don't know is that half dollars minted from 1965–1970 are made of 40% silver, which means they are worth more than their face value. Most of the time, these half dollars sit in banks and collect dust. You can simply approach the teller and ask them if they have any half dollars, exchange cash for rolls, pick out the silver ones and then get the rest of your money back. Even if there are no silver ones, you can simply take back whatever you exchanged and get your cash back. It is a very simple process. You can also use this technique at casinos because many times, casinos have half dollars to pay out small blackjack bets.

The half dollars you are searching for are the 90% silver versions, the 40% silver versions or proof coins. Proof simply means that they were stamped twice at the mint for extra-bold features. They have a sharper image and often have the letter "S" on the front of the coin. When you open a roll, it is easy to see which coins are which by looking at their sides. Post-1970 half dollars are clad and have copper interiors, while the silver versions are mostly silver colored. Check out the image below.

Kennedy Half Dollar comparisons

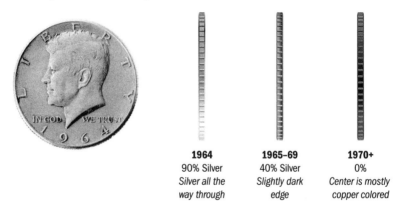

1964	1965–69	1970+
90% Silver	40% Silver	0%
Silver all the way through	*Slightly dark edge*	*Center is mostly copper colored*

You can see how noticeable the differences in coins are. If you are just starting out, it might be good to look at the dates, but once you gain experience, you can simply look at the side of the roll. Even if every roll is clad, you can take everything back and exchange it for cash.

Now here are a few tips . . .

- You don't want to try this with quarters and dimes, because they are extremely circulated. Cashiers and bank tellers, as well as other urban treasure hunters, have been taking them out of circulation, so it's very hard to find silver versions of these coins

- Hand-rolled versions are the best kinds of rolls to hunt for. Usually this means a person recently traded them into the bank and they are more likely to have silver. If you get machine-rolled coins, a busted lip on the roll typically means it has already been searched through and you won't find any silver

- You can increase your odds of finding silver by going to the bank during the holiday season. This is when people exchange their old coins to buy presents for family members

- After you are done coin roll hunting, return the coins to a "dump bank." These are banks that have coin-counting machines, which means you do not have to reroll your coins. You can simply exchange them for cash at that location.

Coin roll hunting can be a lucrative hobby, but it has gained popularity in recent years, especially on the West coast of the U.S. The amount of silver in circulation is slowly diminishing, so be sure to start before the silver is gone.

#4 DETECT METAL WHERE THOUSANDS HAVE BEEN BUT NO ONE HAS SEARCHED

Metal detecting isn't a new hobby. Metal detectors have been around since World War II, when they were used to detect land mines. In the mid-'50s and '60s, metal detecting became a popular hobby as people began searching the grounds of old historic sites in hope of finding valuable relics.

Most "good" metal detecting locations have been gone over thoroughly, so it's very difficult to come up with a decent find these days.

However, a new technology has made it possible to access never-before-searched locations, which has completely revolutionized the way people can find treasures.

What I am referring to is underwater metal detecting. The beach has always been a popular place to search for metals, but engineers have recently developed a fully submersible metal detector that can work in up to 10 feet of water with waterproof and submersible headphones. You can purchase this relatively inexpensive machine and make some incredible finds in places that have never been searched.

I'm not saying you need to go scuba diving to make this work, either. Instead, think about the shallow ponds, beaches or streams around your house. It's possible that in ankle-deep water, there could be throngs of unclaimed treasure.

Many people lose things in water never to be seen again. Jewelry, coins, watches . . . I think we all know someone who has lost something swimming. By taking your metal detector to the local watering hole or beach at low tide, you can come up with some crazy underwater finds that wouldn't be possible without your underwater metal detector. Since this technology is so new, you can be the first one to check out these lucrative locations.

My colleague personally recommends the Garrett AT Pro, which is shown below.

Garrett AT Pro—Full Submersible Metal Detector

This machine has all the specs mentioned above . . . It is fully submersible and has waterproof headphones and an easy-to-read LCD screen. It runs about $600, which is cheaper than other metal detectors with similar or even worse specifications. If you are serious about metal detecting, underwater areas are the new gold mines. Be sure to buy an underwater shovel for easy searching. It is essentially a scoop with small holes that lets the water drain out so you can easily inspect what you find.

There you have it. Four ways to become the modern-day treasure hunter: Become a human metal detector by honing your precious-metal identifying skills. Get free gold at the grocery store by finding lost coins and other items in the Coinstar machine. Get free silver from your bank by coin roll hunting. Or bring a metal detector to never-before-searched areas where people are prone to lose valuables. Hopefully, you can use these tips to score your next big find.

Zach's Income Rating: ★★★☆☆

While urban treasure hunting can be an exhilarating and profitable hobby, it requires ample amount of time, with some hunts yielding no finds. This is a great way to supplement your income as a hobby, but it is not recommended as a sole source of income. For this reason, urban treasure hunting receives three stars.

CHAPTER 31:

AN INCOME TRICK OF THE RICH AND FAMOUS—HOW TO GET A YACHT FOR FREE

Calling all boating enthusiasts! If you currently own a boat or dream of having one, this chapter will reveal a way to significantly cut down your monthly payments and practically give you a boat for free. No matter how much you owe, this technique can generate thousands of dollars a month and is a great way to essentially cancel your monthly payments. Not convinced? Here's how to do it . . .

You can earn a steady flow of income each month by participating in a boat sharing program, similar to other strategies discussed in this book. However, boating is perhaps the most lucrative of all the sharing programs, which make it one of the easiest ways to generate income.

One of the best ways to get into boat sharing is through a business called Boatbound. It's essentially the Airbnb of boating, and allows users to list any boat for charter, whether it's a small fishing boat, catamaran, yacht or sailboat. It's so profitable you can cover your personal boating expenses with only *one or two rentals per month*. Compared with a house rental, which can take weeks to cover your mortgage payment, a boat rental will cover your financing within your first few rentals.

Listing your boat is easy. Simply create a profile on Boatbound's website, **boatbound.co**, by entering your email and password. Then enter the information for the boat you want to list. Enter the make, year and model and Boatbound will give you a recommended listing price for your boat. In the initial signup, you get to choose if you will provide a captain and decide what insurance coverage will apply. For the final step, upload photos, a description and contact information—then you are ready to go.

This requires significantly less effort than chartering your boat through traditional means. You don't have to pay for advertising space or make decisions on how to market. Boatbound does all of the work and connects you with possible renters. So instead of committing hours to a second business, you simply upload your profile and you are ready to go.

Before you decide to list your boat, it is best to have a plan of action. There are many factors that go into a renting experience, so you should carefully consider the following beforehand:

1. Decide what kinds of rentals you want to support. Is your boat going to be rented hourly, by the day or overnight?

2. Make sure you are fully insured. Even though Boatbound provides Geico P2P insurance, make sure your own insurance is fine with the contract.

3. Decide how much experience renters should have. Do you want former captains or copies of boating certificates? More experience means less likelihood of problems down the road.

4. Decide how renters will access your boat. Will you host a meet and greet to give them the key, or will there be a lock box for their convenience?

5. Provide a guide on how to operate the boat. List the controls and show where important objects, such as life jackets, are located. Give emergency contact numbers and have a copy of the rental agreement the users can look over.

After you decide on how you want to conduct rentals, you are ready to get on your way. Renters will leave reviews regarding your service, so give them a great experience to attract more customers. Below are some simple tips to lock in repeat renters:.

1. Give a trial run and show the renters the marina. This allows renters to become comfortable and familiar with their surroundings, but also shows you care about their experience.

2. Show renters where safety equipment, such as life jackets, charts and radio equipment, is located. Again, this raises the comfort level and allows renters to feel more at ease knowing where to look in case of an emergency.

3. Point out pre-existing damages and provide the renters with fuel. After the rental is complete, check the boat for any new damages and make sure it is in good condition. This is good business practice in general and creates a transparent relationship.

Depending on the size and model of your boat, a single one-day rental can bring in anywhere from a couple hundred to several thousand dollars. From small fishing boats to luxury yachts, boatbound.co makes it easy for boat owners looking to make extra cash to connect with those looking to charter. Take a look at these contrasting models located a few miles from my office in Baltimore.

Source: boutbound.co

As you can see, boatbound.co serves almost any kind of boat owner. A small fishing vessel rents for $249 a day. If you rent one out for eight days, that will bring in close to $2,000 a month. Rent out the larger yacht for eight days in a month and you're looking at $40,000—almost half a million a year. If you aren't convinced, take a look at the table below that compares financing with rental income.

Hypothetical rental income

Boat	Purchase price	10-yr financing at 2.0% interest (monthly payment)	Daily rate on Boatbound	Income from 2 rentals a month	Income from 2 rentals a month after paying loan
Boston Whaler	$8,000	$73.61	$249	$498	$424.39
Azimut 68S	$650,000	$5,980.87	$5,000	$10,000	$4,019.13

If you want to own a boat or yacht, renting it out a few days a month will easily cover your financing if you are confident you can find business. In locations like Miami, Annapolis and even Chicago, on the Great Lakes, you should have no problem finding renters looking to charter. Sign up and have your boat pay for itself today.

Check out **boatbound.co** for more information.

Zach's Income Rating: ★★★☆☆

Finance your boat with only two rentals a month—what's not to love? This is a great way to make your boat pay for itself or earn extra income while it sits idly. The problem with this technique is that renters are not guaranteed, especially in a low demand area. So while two rentals might cover your financing, you need to make sure you can find that business. Additionally, if winters are cold, you will need to make up those rentals within the summer months. Therefore, this opportunity receives three stars.

CHAPTER 32:

BRINGING DOWN THE HOUSE: HOW TO TURN THE ODDS IN YOUR FAVOR AT THE LOCAL CASINO

In 2014, the U.S. casino industry brought in over $37 billion in revenue, taken from the pockets of American taxpayers. Casinos have a dicey reputation, but I believe it's all right to spend a few dollars for the sake of entertainment here and there. Gambling only becomes a problem when individuals start frequenting the casino and enter a cycle that makes it impossible to make money in the long run.

Simply put, casino games are not in the player's favor, and most people know this. Nearly every game has a house edge, which means the casino will win at least 51% or more of the time. This may seem like a small advantage, but this edge is what makes casinos billions of dollars over many bets.

Some people attempt to count cards or use "magic systems" to beat the odds. Unfortunately, most casinos know the ways players gain an advantage and have put rules in place to discourage card counting.

What most people don't realize is that there is a single game in the casino that allows you to put the odds in your favor. Best of all, it doesn't require card counting or any other wacky system you may have heard about. If you frequent the casino—it's time to stop playing slots, learn this new game and get your money in with the math on your side.

For those that weren't aware, poker is the one game that can lead to long-term profitable outcomes. Poker has been around for generations, and most people have probably learned a variation in their life. I remember sitting on my grandfather's lap as he taught me five-card draw, the game you see played in old Westerns. Today, there are many different variations of the game, each with their own strategy. No matter what type you play, poker is the only game that you can consistently win at in the casino.

Poker is beatable because instead of playing games that are designed so you lose, you are playing against other people, who are prone to inefficient strategies. Many people think of skill in poker as the ability to bluff and to "read" opponents, but real skill actually consists of basic strategy and mathematical concepts that require only a grade school-level education to understand. Properly bluffing and reading opponents are skills that should be learned after basic strategy is mastered. By using simple math, you can become better than the average player at any casino, which will put the winning odds in your favor.

This chapter isn't going to be an in-depth analysis of poker strategy, but rather a demonstration of why it's the only beatable game in the casino. We will use the most popular game—Texas Hold 'em—as the basis of analysis. Most folks are probably familiar with this game because it was made popular with the ESPN coverage of the World Series of Poker. When an amateur won $2.5 million in 2003, the game exploded and is now the most popular variation in almost every poker room around the world.

In Texas Hold 'em, there are nine–10 players seated at a table with a dealer. There is a dealer button (signifying position) followed by two blinds (forced bets) that rotate clockwise around the table, indicating the order in which players must bet. At the start of each hand, every player receives two cards, known as the hole cards, and this is when the game begins. First, there is a round of betting after receiving the hole cards, and then three cards are placed face up in the middle of the table, which are the community cards, known as the flop. Each player uses the community cards combined with their own to make the best five-card hand. Another round of betting takes place after the flop, and then two more cards are put out, with betting after each. This is known as the turn and river. The diagram below shows the typical setup of a game.

Texas Hold 'em table setup

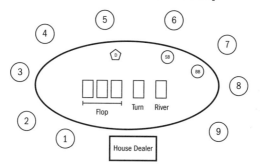

The key to mastering poker starts in the first round of betting, when you receive your hole cards. Some two-card combos are better than others, and this is the first step in beating your opponents. Remember, you use your hole cards to make the best five-card hand with the community cards, so different hole cards have different levels of strength. The rankings of the five-card hands that can be made with the hole cards are shown on the right.

The first step in becoming a winning poker player is to play hole cards that have the mathematical advantage over other hole cards. For example, if you receive two aces and your opponent has a jack and a 10, you already have a made hand and are beating your opponent (one

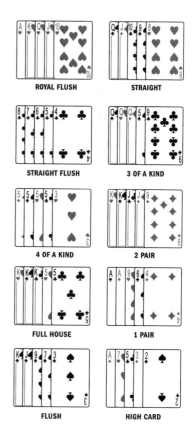

pair vs. high card). Your opponent must improve through the community cards to win, and they must make more than a pair with their holdings. In this exact situation, two aces will beat a jack and a ten 82% of the time, which means you make money in the long run.

Over time, you will come out winning if you consistently put money in when the odds are in your favor. Except instead of a blackjack table that wins 51% of the time, you can get much better odds on your money. Now remember, you won't win every hand, but you will put yourself in a position to win over time, just as the casino does. Sure, a player might get hot and win five blackjack hands in a row, but the house still wins 51% of the time. Over many bets, that 51% brings in billions of dollars in revenue for the casino. It's how they stay open.

The strength of starting hands in Texas Hold 'em can be seen in the 3-D graph below.

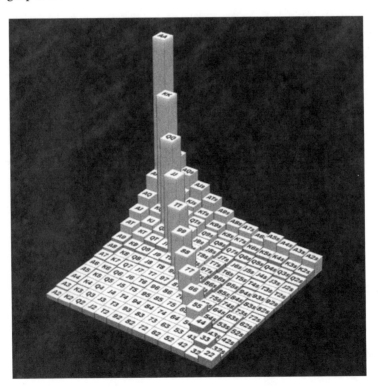

Starting hand strength guide, Source: the-players-edge.com

As you can see, two aces are the strongest hand and will win the majority of times they are played. Now, this isn't saying you should only play when you have aces. Other hands are very strong and can lead to long-term profitability as well. Heck, even playing very weak hands can lead to profitable situations, but that typically requires advanced play and more knowledge about when you have positive expected value. There are going to be times you lose when you have the best hand, but you must remember that if you use this strategy over and over, you'll end up winning money in the long run. The thing about recreational gamblers is that they play many hands because they are impatient or don't know proper game theory, so you can get an edge by exploiting their unprofitable strategy. Simply wait for strong hands and you will have the advantage.

There have been hundreds of books dedicated to mastering poker, and this chapter is only meant to give a basic understanding of why poker is the best game to play in the casino—you can actually come out on top in the long run. If you are interested in reading more on the subject, I recommend Doyle Brunson's *Super System 2* or David Sklansky's *The Theory of Poker*. Both are great introductory reads with enough information to make you better than the average player.

The old motto of Texas Hold 'em goes something like this: It takes five minutes to learn, but a lifetime to master. I don't recommend playing poker to win money if you are new to gambling and have little experience in the casino. However, for those of you that frequent the casino and like playing craps, blackjack, roulette or slots, poker is the better option because it gives you the best odds of making money in the long run.

Zach's Income Rating: ★★☆☆☆

If you frequent the casino, poker is the one game that will put the odds of winning in your favor. I do not recommend playing poker for most—only those that choose to spend time gambling or want to have a fun night on the town. In terms of income, poker receives a two star rating.

CHAPTER 33:

HEALTHY HOBBIES THAT PAY

One of the best ways to make money in retirement is getting your hobby to pay for itself. Rather than picking up a new desk job—do the same things you enjoy doing in your free time with the added bonus of a paycheck.

If you live a healthy and active lifestyle, consider the following opportunities as sources of extra income. Not only will these hobbies put more cash in your wallet, but they will also add to the longevity of your life.

SKI FOR FREE—WITH THE CHANCE TO GET PAID

If you are a seasoned skier or snowboarder and frequently hit the slopes on winter days, becoming a member of the ski patrol is a great way to earn a stream of income with the ability to ski for free.

Skiing is an expensive hobby, and this is a great way to reduce your expenses, make some money and give you the chance to do something positive in your community. You won't get rich ski patrolling, as the majority of positions pay $10–12 dollars an hour. However, with free skiing and extra money, it's a great way to make your hobby pay for itself plus a little extra.

Here are a few things you should know before you hit the slopes:

- Ski patrollers are responsible for the emergency medical and rescue services of participants of snow sports. Most patrollers are recognized through their famed red jacket with white cross. Patrollers are an integral part of the ski community because they are the first to tend to accidents and make sure the trails are safe. In exchange for your service, you get free skiing, first access to the slopes (which means all the fresh powder), a paycheck, plus the camaraderie of an elite group. Compensation varies from resort to resort, but sometimes the perks can also include equipment and guest passes

- The best way to get your foot in the door is through the National Ski Patrol (NSP) organization. This club provides certifications and education for ski patrols across the U.S. Currently, there are 27,000 members from 650 patrols around the country. The NSP administers the Outdoor Emergency Care course, which is an 80–100-hour class that serves as the base-line qualification for ski resorts in the U.S. Some ski resorts will consider you fully qualified if you pass the Outdoor Emergency Care course, while others will require rigorous training and expert talent to join the team. You will also want to make sure that your CPR certifications from the American Heart Association are up to date in order to be considered for the position Check out **www.nsp.org** for more information.

- If you want to go above and beyond the qualifications for the typical patroller, the NSP also offers the following courses for the most challenging conditions:
  - Alpine skiing, snowboarding and Nordic skiing proficiency
  - Toboggan handling (aka Outdoor Emergency Transportation)
  - Mountain Travel and Rescue Levels 1 and 2
  - Avalanche Levels 1 and 2
  - Instructor Development.

Remember, ski patrollers don't make the most money, and in some places, it is volunteer only. But as a volunteer, you will get a free pass and be able to enjoy the responsibility of looking after your mountain.

If you are a regular on the slopes, this might be the perfect way to score some income in retirement. Check with your local resort to see if becoming a ski patroller is right for you.

THE ULTIMATE JOCK RETIREMENT JOB—GET PAID TO WATCH (AND REF) YOUR FAVORITE SPORTS

One of the best retirement jobs out there for old jocks and athletes is to become a sports referee for your local school district. It's fun, good exercise and lets you relive the glory days from the past. Plus, it's a great source of income—a few hours a week can net you a couple hundred dollars.

Each sport has various requirements to get started, so you must check with your local sports authority to figure out how to get involved. For some sports, all you need to do is take a few classes, while others require a more rigorous course load. Once you are certified, you are set to start making income. The payouts can be quite lucrative, so let's take a look at the typical compensation for a high school football referee:

Junior High: $43 per contest
Junior Varsity: $47 per contest
Varsity: $75 per contest

That's solid pay for a couple hours of your time. In addition to the pay per contest, you also receive money in compensation for the miles driven to the game. For a two–three-hour-long football game, this can be a decent way to earn a couple extra bucks while being thrown back into the action of athletics. If you work hard and get lucky enough for the chance to work in collegiate athletics, the pay can increase to over $1,500 a game.

Becoming a referee is a great way to get some extra cash while immersing yourself in the sports that you love. If you are interested, you would most likely start with youth games and then gradually take on more competitive games once you gain experience. Typically, the more competitive, the more lucrative the pay.

For each sport, the method varies on how to enter the officiating world. Soccer has the most direct and organized method, where you take an entry-level class hosted by the United States Soccer Federation to get into peewee soccer games. After displaying competency and taking another training class, you can ref older games and start making bigger paychecks.

Officiating can be exhilarating and allow you to become immersed in entertaining sports contests. If you consider yourself an ex-jock or avid sports fan, this is a perfect way to earn extra money. Becoming a ref helps you stay in shape, improve your conflict negotiations and get outside—all while earning some extra income.

Contact your local sports authority to find out the best way to get involved in the sport of your choice.

CUT YOUR MONTHLY FITNESS FEES—AND GET PAID TO GO TO THE GYM

Another great way to generate income in retirement in a low-stress and healthy environment is to become a personal trainer. If you have experience with working out, using your knowledge and abilities to help others is a great way to earn extra income—plus, a free gym membership.

In particular, senior citizens are becoming more interested in physical exercise, and an older, more experienced trainer might be exactly what they are looking for. Most physical trainers are young and their bodies can handle more impact, but an older client may not be looking to get eye-turning results—instead focusing on flexibility and retaining strength. A retired individual would have the knowledge and experience to know the limitations of other seniors.

Before you can train others, you must get a certification. There are many certifications out there, but one of the best programs, created by the American Council on Exercise, is NCCA accredited and will let you work at almost any gym in the country. The course requires you to invest 80–100 hours of study time over a three–four-month period and will give you all the tools necessary to pass the exam. If you already hold a degree in kinesiology and physiology or have another personal training certification, you can take the test without having to go through the course.

After you pass the test, you must decide what kind of environment you want to work in. Do you want to work in a hot and sweaty body-building gym or an upscale fitness studio? You must define whom you will cater to in order to specialize and bring value as a trainer. A senior citizen who just had hip surgery isn't going to want someone that specializes in powerlifting, just like a bodybuilder won't want a flexibility coach.

After you specialize and develop a client base, you must maintain your certification by earning 20 continuing education credits every two years. Since most seniors are focused on preventing muscle deterioration, improving bone strength and combating the effects of musculoskeletal diseases, a trainer of a similar age might be more accommodating.

For more information, visit **acefitness.org**. This site will give all of the details on how to become a certified trainer.

If weights aren't your style but you are active by other means, such as yoga, consider becoming an instructor in that area of expertise. Again, this source of income should only be considered if you are already practicing the activity, but the income can be extremely lucrative.

Take yoga, for example.

Those familiar with yoga will know that it is more than just stretching or odd poses. Yoga encompasses a lifestyle, and most students want their teacher to be someone who follows the proper path. Regular practice, eating healthy and abstaining from substance abuse are necessary to portray the ideal yoga instructor and maintain clients. Being a yoga instructor takes dedication, but the benefits range from a healthier body and mind to a lucrative source of income. In fact, the average pay for a yoga instructor is $25 an hour. Most instructors are certified through **yogaalliance.org**, so check out their website for how to start.

Once you are up and running, check out **theyogipreneur.com**. This website is a great resource on how to build your yoga business. It contains many articles on how to attract and maintain customers—specifically targeted for yoga instructors.

If you are a healthy individual looking to make extra income, turn your lifestyle hobbies into moneymaking businesses. These opportunities require more dedication than others mentioned in this book, but they are fun and healthy and allow for a greater stream of income.

Zach's Income Rating: ★★★☆☆

These are great hobbies that have the potential to not only add dollars to your pocket, but also years to your life! If you are an avid skier, join the ski patrol to earn income while having your hobby pay for itself. Or, continue your own fitness goals by becoming a personal trainer and helping others. These sources of income require time, dedication and expertise. For that reason, these opportunities receive an income rating of three stars.

CHAPTER 34:

MAKE MONEY FROM YOUR BED EACH MONTH

Let me get straight to the point. This chapter isn't going to be one of the most glamorous ways to make money. It can be tedious and take some time to result in anything of worth, but it's a strategy you can use at home even if you are bedbound due to illness.

All it requires is your time and some patience. I've included this chapter for those who have trouble leaving the house and want a little extra spending money each month. This strategy can land you a couple hundred dollars a month, a perfect amount of spending money if you are restricted from earning in other ways.

You may have heard online surveys can land you some income, but usually, the surveys are long, the websites lie about how much time it takes and the compensation is not worth it.

However, there are a few websites that stand out above the rest. The times are accurate, the amount of compensation ranges and sites provides other means to make money besides filling out surveys, including signing up for offers or testing out products.

One of the sites that offer the greatest return for your time is **swagbucks.com**. Setting up an account takes less than five minutes, and you can start earning points immediately. Compared with other paid survey sites, Swagbucks is much better than the rest.

The way it works is simple. For each task or survey you complete, you are awarded a certain number of points, or Swagbucks. These points can be exchanged for a variety of prepaid gift cards that are sent to your home. Examples include prepaid Visa cards and specialty cards for websites such as Amazon.

Besides answering surveys, you can earn points by watching videos or signing up for special internet offers. For example, answering a one-question poll might land you 10 cents, while answering a detailed marketing survey could land you a couple dollars. The Swagbucks website is very user friendly and makes it easy to see how many points you have accumulated and what the different tasks are worth. There are also incentives to hit daily goals so you can be rewarded with extra points.

Swagbucks is transparent with its surveys and lets you know how your information is going to be used. It is fairly secure. The only issue is that Swagbucks contains links to other websites, which may have different privacy policies. Be sure to use caution when clicking on links that take you to other websites.

While it's not glamorous, a few hours each day can land you some extra income each month. Swagbucks is a viable option for making income if you spend most of your time at home and want more spending money.

Check out swagbucks.com for more information.

Zach's Income Rating: ★★★☆☆

Taking online surveys is time consuming and usually there are better ways to earn income with the same amount of effort. However, if you are stuck at home, Swagbucks is a viable way to earn a couple extra dollars.

CHAPTER 35:

HOW TO TURN EXTREME COUPONING INTO CASH

There is an elite group of shoppers that have figured out how to milk their shopping experiences to the max. They not only get items for free, but also have stores literally hand out cash to them. At first, this concept seems ridiculous, but in this chapter, I will show how anyone can *make money* while shopping.

For skeptical readers, I encourage you to look up the show *Extreme Couponing*, which is a good example of how individuals are able to get loads of items for pennies on the dollar. However, this book is about income, and great deals are only a bonus of what we are here to accomplish.

Through extreme couponing, you can actually make money on the products you purchase. In the past, this technique required hours of research and effort to be successful. You needed to be well versed in the loopholes in store policies and factory coupons to make it possible.

However, in today's computer age, finding these "moneymakers" requires much less effort to pull off. In fact, I'll reveal a source that gives that information for free.

It is a website that contains information on extreme deals, and some of these deals can actually make you money after you complete the transaction. Normally, it takes a combination of store coupons, factory coupons and mail-in rebates, but these deals are easy to get once you know how.

There is an army of nerds constantly looking for deals, and when one comes up, they post it to **slickdeals.net**. This website contains deals from every industry imaginable, and today, I'd like to show you how to use this website to score items for free, plus make some income on those purchases. Slickdeals not only contains crazy ways to make money with coupons, but also lists great discounts on things you may be looking for. Half off laptops, brand-name shoes for a third of their retail price . . . You name it and Slickdeals has it.

However, while great deals are always a bonus, we want to make money. So to find the moneymaking coupons, follow these steps:

Step 1: Go to slickdeals.net. You will see the screen below as the home page:

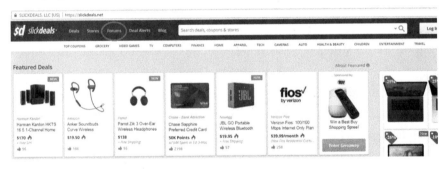

Step 2: Hover your mouse over the "Forums" section and you will see "Hot Deals" under the "Deals" category. Click on "Hot Deals."

Step 3: Profit. The "Hot Deals" home page will look something like the screen below:

Those blue links in the grey shaded area are some of the best discounts in the U.S., but you have still have to search for the income opportunities.

Look for links that include the word "moneymaker," or "MM" for short. This means that if you partake in the deal and complete all the steps, you will actually make money.

Most of the time, these deals require a store sale combined with a factory coupon or mail-in rebate.

It's that simple!

You can use this trick to score household items for free, plus make some extra income. These deals won't be around all the time, so check regularly to find the most recent and up-to-date deals. By no stretch of the imagination could monitoring these sites turn into real cash in your pocket.

And that's how you turn extreme couponing into cash. Before the internet, these deals were nearly impossible to find, and only the most savvy couponers were able to score. Nowadays, anyone can do it. This technique won't be the most lucrative income-generating strategy, but you'll be able to shop for free and get paid to do so.

Zach's Income Rating: ★★★☆☆

Getting paid to shop is one of the most satisfying experiences. While Fatwallet and slickdeals have already found the money making opportunities, you still have to find the appropriate coupons and travel to the store to get the deal. In some cases, the deal might be canceled, or the proper store could be hours away. For that reason, this opportunity receives three stars.

Hey, Zach Scheidt here. Thanks for reading my book!

Congrats on making it to the end!

Since you are a special reader who is serious about their income, I'd like to give a crazy deal on Lifetime Income Report that you'd only find by finishing this book.

Keep this ridiculous 'secret' just between you and me.

This is a special book-only offer you'll only find by going to the website below.

Go to **sites.agorafinancial.com/LIR/BigBookSurvey** for more information.

Here's to growing your income,

Zach Scheidt